Library of Public Policy and Public Administration

Volume 20

Around the world there are challenges to the way we administer government. Some of these have to do with brute force that is backed by self-interest. However, there are those intrepid souls who think we are all better than this. This series of monographs and edited collections of original essays seeks to explore the very best way that governments can execute their sovereign duties within the sphere of ethically-based public policy that recognizes human rights and the autonomy of its citizens.

Proposals to the series can include policy questions that are nationally or internationally situated. For example, regional migration from victims of war, terrorism, police integrity, political corruption, the intersection between politics and public health, hunger, clean water and sanitation, global warming, treatment of the "other" nationally and internationally, and issues of distributive justice and human rights.

Proposals that discuss systemic changes in the structure of government solutions will also be considered. These include *corruption and anti-corruption, bribery, nepotism,* and *effective systems design.*

Series benchmark: 110,000-150,000 words. Special books can be somewhat longer.

Wanda Teays

Solitary Confinement

Philosophical Perspectives

Springer

Wanda Teays
Philosophy
Mount Saint Mary's University
Los Angeles, CA, USA

ISSN 1566-7669
Library of Public Policy and Public Administration
ISBN 978-3-031-96565-4   ISBN 978-3-031-96566-1 (eBook)
https://doi.org/10.1007/978-3-031-96566-1

This Springer imprint is published by the registered company Springer Nature Switzerland AG
The registered company address is: Gewerbestrasse 11, 6330 Cham, Switzerland

Acknowledgments

Thank you, Travis Holloway, publishing editor at Springer. I am grateful for your support and encouragement. Thanks also to Michael Boylan for *his* support and encouragement. And thank you Willow Bunu for your research and reference skills. It is a blessing to have people believe in you.

Finally, let us not forget you, the reader, for giving your time and attention to this most important issue. Together we can make a difference and change this abusive practice of solitary confinement.

Justice leaves its mark across space and time. The past travels with us, a silent companion as we navigate the present and create the future.

Competing Interests The author has no competing interests to declare that are relevant to the content of this manuscript.

Contents

Part I
Introduction

Chapter 1
Introduction

Contents

There's right and there's wrong. Right is better. John McCain got it right when he said,

> It's an awful thing solitary. … It crushes your spirit and weakens your resistance more effectively than any other form of mistreatment. (Fetig 2011)

To look at the widespread use of this practice, you would think there's not much disagreement—and not much objectionable—to "absolute solitude," as sociologist Alexis de Tocqueville called it in 1831. After touring a New York prison, he concluded solitary confinement had no reformative value (Marcus 2012). The reality is that solitary confinement is about the worst punishment imaginable.

"It's impossible to exaggerate how much the company of another human being means when you've been cut off from the world and stripped of your rights and freedom," said Sarah Shourd. Imprisoned by the Iranian government after she and two friends went hiking near the border of Iraqi Kurdistan, Shourd spent 14 months in an Iranian prison—almost a year of that in solitary confinement. She said that, after just 2 months in solitary, her "mind began to slip." She experienced hallucinations and started beating the walls of her cell until her knuckles bled (as noted by Feting 2011).

Journalist Dashka Slater says of the "punitive American model" that "our approach is ineffective, costly, and cruel" (2017, p. 331). Thousands upon thousands of people—from children and juveniles to adults, from citizens to immigrants,

W. Teays, *Solitary Confinement*, Library of Public Policy and Public Administration 20, https://doi.org/10.1007/978-3-031-96566-1_1

from inmates to detainees and suspected terrorists, from young to old—have been subjected to solitary. In other words, a broad spectrum of people have been its victims. No other mistreatment compares.

We might wonder: what is so wrong with prolonged solitude? For centuries monks and other religious seekers have meditated day in and day out, all alone for hours on end. They do not seem to suffer from the solitude they willingly adopted. True, but one major difference is the monks and seekers have had a community in the background, and this is a path they've chosen. Theirs is not an "absolute solitude" that is prolonged and unbounded.

Quakers turned to solitary confinement in the 1800's as a vehicle of reformation. They mistakenly assumed this would transform offenders by using the solitude to read the Bible, absorb its wisdom, and change their ways. Unfortunately, that was not to be—and it has remained an unattainable goal. Whether it be days or decades, being stuck in a cell, isolated from human contact, Bible or no Bible—the result is a total disaster. Experts have testified to its harms and have called for its elimination.

Basically, solitary confinement is a form of shunning by cutting off all human contact. The consequences of such social isolation are devastating, with long-lasting effects. This is particularly the case with prolonged solitary, which is a vehicle to suicidal depression. Self-destruction results. As we will see in this book, no good can come of it.

Lead investigator of a study of solitary confinement, Katherine Peeler, gave testimony on April 16, 2024 before the U.S. Senate Committee on the Judiciary on the health impacts of solitary confinement. Although she concentrated on immigrant detention, her assessment applies across the board. She made the following points (2024):

- *Solitary Confinement Beyond 15 Days Has Been Deemed Torture*

- Prolonged solitary, as defined by the United Nations is a period of solitary confinement in excess of fifteen days. According to the U.N. that constitutes torture.
- *Solitary Confinement Use is Widespread*
- A 2023 report showed that 122,000 people were held in solitary in U.S. prisons and jails on a given day in 2019; a separate study of U.S. prisons showed that 41,000 people were in solitary confinement for 22 hours or more per day for at least 15 days or more in July 2021, and most recently, a 2024 study showed that 8% of Bureau of Prisons inmates are in solitary confinement.
- As for U.S. Immigration and Customs Enforcement (ICE) detention: From 2018–2023, ICE placed people in solitary confinement over 14,000 times for an average duration of 27 days.
- *Solitary Confinement is Detrimental to Health*
- Subjects reported anxiety, depression, panic attacks, hallucinations, and other mental health conditions. A February2024 report from the Bureau of Prisons state that 46%—almost half—of Bureau of Prisons suicides take place in solitary confinement.
- *Solitary Confinement is Used Indiscriminately, is Under-Reported, and thus Harms Many More than We Know*

- Solitary confinement is used punitively, administratively, protectively (e.g., of LGBQT inmates), as medical isolation, and as a form of retaliation.
- *Alternatives to Solitary Confinement Exist*
- Combined better discretion about who *might* need solitary confinement with specific techniques to assist someone who might need de-escalation or protection, this program resulted in an almost 75% decrease in the use of solitary confinement between 2016–2020.
- *In Brief:*

- Solitary confinement for any amount of time causes severe and long-lasting mental and physical health harms. We must urgently eliminate this practice completely in the United States.

As Maria Morris, senior staff attorney with American Civil Liberties Union's National Prison Project, said: "It's important to understand just how dangerous and harmful solitary confinement is" (ACLU 2024). To understand the dangers and harms of solitary confinement, we need to get a sense of the territory. Let's take a moment to see the recipients of this practice.

1.1 Adults in Prisons and Jails

"I ended up losing my mind for two weeks, even talking to myself. I thought about suicide. I still have those thoughts," lamented a man who had been subjected to solitary (Peeler 2024). His experience is not unique; all too many held in solitary convey similar feelings.

In such extreme isolation, segregated in an 8x10 windowless space, with only a slab to sleep on, a toilet and sink and not even a chair to sit in—the "living" conditions are about as grim as you can picture. It is no wonder you would think your mind was slipping away. Not surprisingly, the sense of losing your mind can result in paranoia and fear of vulnerability. As one victim of solitary expressed, "Sometimes I feel like someone is following me and I'm afraid they'll take me to solitary confinement" (Peeler 2024). It is certainly not something you would ever want to repeat. However, repeated trips to solitary are all too common. Here is the reality:

> Individuals in solitary confinement spend 22 to 24 hours a day locked in small, often windowless cells, without human contact, and usually without work, education, or programming of any kind. This type of isolation and sensory deprivation has been shown to cause extreme anguish and, in many cases, lasting psychological damage to those who endure it (Solitary Watch-a 2024).

Prolonged solitary confinement fits the definition of torture according to the United Nations and other human rights associations—see Chap. 14 on principles and ethics codes. If you don't think it is torture, just picture yourself in a tiny, windowless space, cut off from human contact, without even a window to see outside, and nothing whatsoever to read or listen to. Picture this as your existence for days, weeks, months—or years. It's a recipe for suicidal depression and many people simply give up.

1.2 Women in Detention

There are many more men in prison than women. That said, the incarcerated female population has grown twice as fast from 1980 to 2020 (Solitary Watch-b 2024). Incarcerated journalist Elizabeth Hawes found that many women sent to solitary were punished for minor issues like singing, braiding hair, walking backwards in the courtyards, loitering, placing unauthorized phone calls, and hugging other incarcerated women (Solitary Watch-b 2024).

Come on! Do those sound like punishable acts? *Any* punishment for singing, braiding hair, and the like seems out of line. That it could result in solitary confinement is incomprehensible.

1.3 Juvenile Detention

Juvenile detention facilities ("youth prisons") have been in the spotlight lately, with states considering their role and existence. There are good reasons for this appraisal, considering the issues. Take this example that Valerie Kiebala, managing editor of Solitary Watch points out:

> At the Lincoln Hills School for Boys (a Wisconsin juvenile correctional facility) two entire buildings exist to hold children in solitary confinement for 22 to 23 hours a day. Each unit has two-dozen isolation cells, which measure seven by ten feet and contain only a metal sink, a toilet, and a mattress. In the smaller sister facility one wing is reserved for solitary confinement. The lights in these cells stay lit 24 hours a day. (Kiebala 2017)

"Children as young as 14 are sent to these units at the discretion of the staff for disciplinary reasons, including minor rule violations, or for an "asserted security reason" (Kiebala 2017). In addition:

> For those in solitary, class time may be cut down to less than an hour per day, during which the students may have their wrists cuffed to a canvas belt around their waist…the facilities often keep them handcuffed during their one-hour breaks from solitary confinement, sometimes even during their showers. (Kiebala 2017)

A former guard said the environment at these Wisconsin youth prisons was like "the ninth circle of Hell" (Kiebala 2017). Think of Dante's *Inferno.* If that's not a wake-up call nothing is.

The good news is that change is in the air. In 2023 California took steps to dismantle their youth prisons. Journalists James Rainey and James Queally report that, "After a two-year wind-down, California is in the final weeks of closing its notoriously grim youth prison system, a landmark moment that arrives as juvenile crime hovers at near-record lows and state leaders call for a shift in focus from punishment to rehabilitation" (2023).

Furthermore, "the eleven lockups the Division of Juvenile Justice once operated will be replaced by an array of programs devised by probation departments in California's 58 counties — many of which have little experience with the long-term care of young people convicted of serious crimes" (Rainey and Queally 2023). Hopefully the lack of experience can be overcome. In any case, closing the juvenile prisons is a step in the right direction.

The American Psychological Association (APA) would echo that recommendation. Journalist Sara Vogel (2024) notes that the APA has adopted a resolution that calls for prohibiting children from being placed in solitary confinement, except for emergencies where a young person is in immediate danger of serious physical harm to themselves and others.

1.4 Schools

There must be an awful lot of behavioral issues in schools, given the extent solitary confinement is put to use. Seclusion rooms—note the euphemism—are used to hold children in solitary confinement in schools around the world. Professor Dan Moshenberg (2020) explains:

> Seclusion is vaguely defined by the U.S. Department of Education's Office of Civil Rights as "involuntarily confining a student alone in a room or area from which he or she cannot physically leave." There are no federal regulations concerning the design or use of seclusion rooms. Some facilities use janitorial closets; others use booths or padded, windowless cells. Seclusion rooms are often referred to as "time out spaces" or "last resort." But to the children sent there, the rooms often feel like prisons.

These closets or other seclusion rooms do not just "feel like" prisons—they function like them too. They are vehicles of power and oppression, as Michel Foucault would contend (see Chap. 9) As the following case illustrates, their effect can be devastating:

> In 2004, 13-year-old Jonathan King was confined to a windowless, 8' x 8' concrete block room 19 times over a 29-day period at Alpine Program, a Georgia school for students with behavioral problems. During these stints in the "time-out" room, he spent an average of 95 minutes alone with no furniture, food, water, or bathroom access. On November 15, 2004, King hanged himself in the isolation room. (Moshenberg 2020)

That was in Georgia. Other states face the same issues with the misuse of segregation and isolation of children of all ages. It is a shocking situation. Look at the statistics Moshenberg (2020) cites for the state of Maine: "In May of [2020] Disability Rights Maine released a report finding that restraint and seclusion were used 20,000 times in Maine schools in 2018—*once every five minutes* that school was in session." Who was targeted? The majority of seclusions occurred in "special purpose private schools for children with disabilities" (Moshenberg 2020).

1.5 ICE Detention

"We have found widespread use, and misuse, of solitary confinement in ICE detention," cites Katherine Peeler in her testimony to the U.S. Senate Committee on the Judiciary (2024).

Peeler's assessment is in accordance with the 2019 report by the International Consortium of Investigative Journalists. They found that between 2012 and 2017 solitary was used to punish immigrants for offenses as minor as consensual kissing and to segregate hunger strikers, LGBTQ detainees and people with disabilities (Wolfe 2019). They concluded, says Solitary Watch contributor Abram Wolfe, that "U.S. immigration authorities have been misusing and overusing solitary confinement in detention centers housing tens of thousands of immigrants from around the world" (Wolfe 2019).

As we can see from solitary confinement being used so widely, this is not an insignificant issue. It affects thousands of people around the world, with the United States being a major offender. The time for change is long overdue. Here's where the major philosophers and contemporary ethicists can help us. We have much to gain by examining their philosophical perspectives and applying them to solitary confinement. That is the focus of this book. Their words of wisdom can guide us as we venture into this territory.

1.6 The Bigger Picture

Before we go deeper into solitary confinement, we should note that much of its use takes place in prisons, jails, and detention facilities. Angela Y. Davis and others have advocated the abolition of such confinement. Would we need prisons if drug use, poverty, medical care, education and mental healthcare were addressed? Mostly not at all. "Why do we take prison for granted?" she asks. As Davis notes, we are "often afraid to face the realities they produce" (2003, p. 15). The focus of this book is on one of those realities—solitary confinement—which is used and abused.

Indeed, prisons are "the main form of punishment," Davis points out (2003, p. 37). Solitary confinement is one way that punishment is put to use. She rightly raises concerns about the role prisons play in our society. My focus is on one abusive aspect of prisons and other institutions—namely solitary confinement with its isolation and segregation. That said, the broader concerns regarding prisons would be good to keep in mind.

Davis, not surprisingly, asserts that "solitary confinement—next to torture, or as a form of torture—is considered the worst form of punishment imaginable" (2003, pp. 47–48). She cites Charles Dickens' view that solitary confinement is "cruel and wrong" Furthermore,"I [Charles Dickins] believe that very few men are capable of estimating the immense amount of torture and agony that this dreadful punishment, prolonged for years, inflicts upon the sufferers" (Quoted by Davis 2003, p. 48).

Davis has had considerable influence in asking "Are prisons obsolete?" Similarly, I would ask "Is solitary confinement obsolete?" In the chapters ahead, I draw from historical and contemporary philosophical perspectives to argue that it should be.

1.7 Structure of this Book

There are five parts to this book:

- Part I: Introduction to the Text

  Chap. 1: Introduction

- Part II: The Practice

  Chap. 2: Overview
  Chap. 3: Hoods and Sandbags

- Part III: Historical Perspectives

  Chap. 4: Jeremy Bentham: The Panopticon
  Chap. 5: John Stuart Mill: On Societal Benefits
  Chap. 6: Immanuel Kant: On Punishment
  Chap. 7: Aristotle: On Reformation and Rehabilitation
  Chap. 8: John Rawls: On Justice

- Part IV: Contemporary Perspectives

  Chap. 9: Michel Foucault: Punishment and Power
  Chap. 10: Tom L. Beauchamp and James F. Childress: Principles of Biomedical Ethics
  Chap. 11: Michael Boylan: The Impact of Worldviews
  Chap. 12: Nel Noddings: The Components of Evil
  Chap. 13: Claudia Card: The Atrocity Paradigm

- Part V: Principles and Ethics Codes

  Chap. 14: Principles and Ethics Codes
  Chap. 15: Recommendations

References

ACLU Press Release. 2024, April 16. Ahead of U.S. Senate Hearing on Solitary Confinement, Survivors of Solitary Confinement & Allies Rallied to Urge President Biden and Congress to Enact the End Solitary Confinement Act. *American Civil Liberties Union* (ACLU). https://www.aclu.org/press-releases/ahead-of-u-s-senate-hearing-on-solitary-confinement-survivors-of-solitary-confinement-allies-rallied-to-urge-president-biden-and-congress-to-enact-the-end-solitary-confinement-act

Davis, Angela Y. 2003. *Are prisons obsolete?* New York: Seven Stories Press.
Feting, Amy. 2011, November 7. Solitary confinement destroys all kinds of people. ACLU. https://www.aclu.org/news/smart-justice/solitary-confinement-destroys-all-kinds-people
Kiebala, Valerie. 2017, February 22. Wisconsin Juvenile Prisons, children face a nightmare of solitary confinement. *Solitary Watch.* https://solitarywatch.org/2017/02/22/at-wisconsin-juvenile-prisons-children-face-a-nightmare-of-solitary-confinement-and-abuse/
Marcus, Ruth. 2012, October 17. Solitary confinement: The cruelest punishment. *Seattle Times.* https://www.seattletimes.com/opinion/solitary-confinement-the-cruelest-punishment/
Moshenberg, Dan. 2020, January 30. For vulnerable children, the school day can include solitary confinement. *Solitary Watch.* https://solitarywatch.org/2020/01/30/for-vulnerable-children-the-school-day-can-include-solitary-confinement/
Peeler, Katherine. 2024, April 16. Legacy of harm: Eliminating the abuse of solitary confinement: Testimony. U.S. Senate Committee on the Judiciary. https://www.judiciary.senate.gov/committee-activity/hearings/legacy-of-harm-eliminating-the-abuse-of-solitary-confinement
Rainey, James and James Queally. 2023, June 2. California is closing its last youth prisons. Will what replaces them be worse? *Los Angeles Times.*
Slater, Dashka. 2017. North Dakota's Norway experiment. In *Dismantling mass incarceration: A handbook for change*, ed. Premal Dharia, James Forman Jr., and Maria Hawilo. New York: Farrah, Straus, and Giroux.
Solitary Watch-a. 2024. Lifelines to solitary. *Solitary Watch.* https://solitarywatch.org/about-lifelines/
Solitary Watch-b. 2024. Women in solitary confinement. Solitary Watch Fact Sheet #8. https://solitarywatch.org/wp-content/uploads/2024/08/SW-Fact-Sheet-8-Women-in-Solitary-Davis20240826.pdf
Vogel, Sara. 2024, March 13. American Psychological Association resolution calls for a ban on youth solitary. *Solitary Watch.* https://solitarywatch.org/2024/03/13/american-psychological-association-resolution-calls-for-ban-on-youth-solitaryand-other-news-on-solitary-confinement-this-week/
Wolfe, Abram. 2019, July 30. Solitary confinement in immigration detention is a grim reality—And only likely to get worse. *Solitary Watch.* https://solitarywatch.org/2019/07/30/solitary-confinement-in-immigration-detention-is-a-grim-reality-and-only-likely-to-get-worse/

Part II
The Practice

Chapter 2
Overview

Contents

2.1 Introduction

It is no mistake on Nel Noddings' part to consider isolation a manifestation of evil. The utter cruelty of confining another person to a cell, cage, or box boggles the mind. That it can go on for years or even decades is unimaginable. Where was the

---

Teays, Wanda. 2019. "Solitary Confinement." In *Doctors and Torture: Medicine at the Crossroads*, Springer. Used with permission.

W. Teays, *Solitary Confinement*, Library of Public Policy and Public Administration 20, https://doi.org/10.1007/978-3-031-96566-1_2

outcry when Zacarias Moussaoui was sentenced to life in prison in solitary confinement with no possibility of parole for his role in the attacks on 9/11?

The fantasy of the Quakers who thought solitary confinement would purify the soul and be an effective form of rehabilitation has been shown to be groundless. That it has continued to the present day and is commonly used in prisons and detention centers shows how misguided is this policy and how urgent is the need to put an end to it.

Let's assume for the moment that there could be therapeutic benefits to a short period of isolation. If that were the case, we would need to clarify what they are and whether they outweigh the long-term risks. The practice needs to be assessed by medical professionals to fully grasp the potential harms and consider the alternatives.

Professors of Medicine Cyrus Ahalt and Brie Williams (2016) are right on track in raising this concern: "Aside from conducting some important studies that have linked even relatively brief isolation to worsening mental health, the medical community has been largely absent from the national debate over solitary confinement. That absence is conspicuous."

It's conspicuous and it needs to change. This is particularly so, given the rampant misuse of the practice. We see this with the number of minor infractions that result in "segregation" (= solitary).

2.2 The Misuse of Solitary

Researcher Joshua Manson cites examples from a United Nation's report.

> In both the U.S. immigration and detention and federal prison systems, for example, people can be held in solitary confinement for the sole reason that they will be released, removed, or transferred within 24 hours. Also under U.S. federal law, people can be held in solitary confinement if they are HIV-positive and there is "reliable evidence" that they may "pose a health risk" to others.
>
> In California, people may be subject to isolation just because they are "a relative or associate of a staff member." In Pennsylvania, people may be subject to solitary confinement, against their will and consent, because they are "at a high risk of sexual victimization" if there exists no "alternative means of separation from the likely abuser." Also in Pennsylvania, people may be subject to solitary confinement simply because "there is no other appropriate bed space." (Manson 2016)

And so on. You don't have to be a danger to others to end up in solitary confinement, contrary to what we might think. This is particularly disturbing considering the potential harms of being placed in solitary for even short periods. It can cause long-lasting trauma, mental suffering, and psychological harm.

Solitary can also heighten the risk of suicide. We see this, for example, with the case of Jack Letts. A British-Canadian man who went off to Syria to join ISIS, Letts was captured and held in prison by Kurdish authorities. He ended up in solitary.

> He told the [Canadian] consular official that he had attempted suicide after his first month in solitary confinement but was found in time by his Kurdish guards. "I started to go insane

> and talk to myself and I thought dying was better than my mother seeing me insane," Letts said. "So I tried to hang myself." He has since been allowed to live in a cell with other prisoners. (Brewster 2018)

Jack Letts's reaction to solitary matches the experience of one after another after another. We can see this in the following six cases—the use of solitary on a lawyer, a detainee, two hostages, three prisoners, three on Death Row, and juveniles in detention in Louisiana. Each case paints a bleak picture of the use of solitary confinement.

2.2.1 *First Case: Lawyer Xie Yanyi*

Xie Yanyi had spent much of his career in China representing clients in sensitive legal cases involving victims of official corruption, police violence or religious persecution. John Sudworth (2017) of the BBC reports on China's "war on law":

> The crackdown on China's already beleaguered human rights field began in mid 2015, halfway through Xi Jinping's first term. Now, anointed in office for a second term by the Communist Party Congress that ended this week, it stands as one of his most gloomy legacies. In total, more than 300 lawyers, legal assistants and activists have been brought in for questioning, with more than two dozen pursued as formal investigations.

Xie Yanyi, one of those arrested, said he didn't see sunlight for 6 months and that he was kept in a stress position and crouched on a low stool from 6:00 in the morning until 10:00 at night. He elaborates:

> After 15 days like this, [he said], his legs went numb, and he had difficulty urinating. At times he was denied food and was beaten …But harder to bear was the time spent in solitary confinement, he asserts. "I was kept alone in a small room and saw no daylight for half a year. I had nothing to read, nothing to do but to sit on that low stool." In his view, "People could go mad in that situation. I was isolated from the world. This is torture—the isolation is more painful than being beaten." (Sudworth 2017)

2.2.2 *Second Case: Detainee Jose Padilla*

Detainee and American citizen Jose Padilla was held over three years in solitary confinement. The conditions were harsh: His windows were blacked out; there was no clock or calendar and only a steel platform to sleep on (no mattress) before having access to legal counsel (Sontag 2006).

Two psychiatrists and a psychologist who conducted examinations of Padilla contend that both his extended detention in solitary and interrogation left him with severe mental disabilities. All three say he may never recover. In their opinion, "Padilla's ordeal in the brig was so psychologically unsettling that it has left him terrorized. Any reminder of the ordeal through questions by his lawyers or others triggers a recurrence of the disorganizing terror Padilla experienced" (Richey 2007).

2.2.3 *Third Case: Hostages Terry Anderson and Frank Reed*

Journalist Terry Anderson was covering Lebanon's civil war of 1975–90 when he was kidnapped along with other foreigners. He was released in 1991 after being held prisoner in an underground dungeon for six-and-a-half years (History.com 2009).

Fellow hostage Frank Reed, an American private-school director, was held in solitary confinement for 4 months before being put in with Anderson. Surgeon and public health commentator Atul Gawande reports on Reed's condition: "By then, Reed had become severely withdrawn. He lay motionless for hours facing a wall, semi-catatonic. He could not follow the guards' simplest instructions. Released after three and a half years, Reed ultimately required admission to a psychiatric hospital" (2009).

Anderson did not fare so well either:

> He missed people terribly, especially his fiancée and his family. He was despondent and depressed … A month into his confinement, he recalled in his memoir, "The mind is a blank. Jesus, I always thought I was smart. Where are all the things I learned, the books I read, the poems I memorized? There's nothing there, just a formless, gray-black misery. My mind's gone dead. God, help me." One day, three years into his ordeal, he snapped. He walked over to a wall and began beating his forehead against it, dozens of times. His head was smashed and bleeding before the guards were able to stop him. (Gawande 2009)

2.2.4 *Fourth Case: Prisoners Robert King, Herman Wallace, and Albert Woodfox, aka "the Angola Three"*

The three Black Panther-activists were convicted in the early 1970's of a prison guard's murder (they claimed they were framed). Each spent decades in solitary—King 29 years, Wallace 41 years, and Woodfox 43 years, the longest in US history. King commented on the conditions:

> The cells were pretty bare, and they were maybe about … 3 feet wide and about 6 feet long. It was almost like it was in a tomb, and there was a slab of concrete that you slept on. You ate three meals a day — you had two slices of bread each meal. During the wintertime, you froze, and during summertime, you were overheated. But in any event, you were starved. (Kennedy 2016)

Wallace died three days after his release in 2013. Woodfox was freed February 19, 2016 and died August 4, 2022, from complications of Covid-19. In a February 2016 interview with *The Guardian (UK),* Woodfox remarked on the brutality of solitary:

> Some of the guys found the pressure so great that they just laid down in a fetal position and stopped communicating with anybody. I've seen other guys who just want to talk and make

> noise, guys who want to scream. Breaking up manifests itself in any number of ways in individuals." (Pilkington 2016)

As for himself, Woodfox observed that,

> The panic attacks started with sweating. You sweat and you can't stop. You become soaking wet—you are asleep in your bunk and everything is soaking wet. Then when the claustrophobia starts it feels like the atmosphere is pressing down on you. That was hard. I used to talk to myself to convince myself I was strong enough to survive, just to hold on to my sanity until the feeling went away. (Pilkington 2016)

2.2.5 *Fifth Case: Death Row Convicts Marcus Hamilton, Winthrop Eaton and Michael Perry*

Convicted of first-degree murder in Louisiana and sentenced to death, all three men have been in solitary confinement for over 25 years. They aren't the only ones: According to journalist Liam Stack, in 2017 seventy-one prisoners sentenced to death in Louisiana we're being held in solitary confinement at the Angola state penitentiary (2017).

> They spend 23 hours a day in windowless concrete cells that measure 8 by 10 feet. They are allowed to leave the cell for one hour each day to shower, make phone calls or walk along the tiered walkway beside their cells. Three times a week, they can use that hour to go outside to sit in a small outdoor cage. (Stack 2017)

Evidently "a lot, if not most" of the states that have the death penalty house their death row inmates in solitary confinement according to Betsy Ginsberg, the director of the civil rights clinic at the Benjamin N. Cardozo School of Law (Stack 2017).

The damaging effects of prolonged solitary confinement on the mental and physical health of prisoners have been well established, as Stack points out. Social psychologist Craig Haney notes that even those with no history of mental illness were engaged in a "constant, ongoing struggle to maintain their sanity." In addition, "These conditions predictably can impair the psychological functioning of the prisoners who are subjected to them," he [observed]. "For some prisoners, these impairments can be permanent and life-threatening" (as noted by Stack 2017).

2.2.6 *Sixth Case: Juveniles in Detention*

"Being in isolation to me felt like I was on an island all alone, dying a slow death from the inside out." So spoke a child held in U.S. juvenile detention, as Ian Kysel (2012) of Human Rights Watch notes. The reality is that minors from 14–20 years old are being held in solitary. Kysel (2012) reports:

> New York City officials told me that more than 14 per cent of 16 to18 year olds in city jails in the most recent fiscal year were held in solitary confinement to punish them. The average

> stay was 43 days – longer than for adults. In Pennsylvania's prison facility for "youthful offenders", which holds young people ranging from age 14 to their early 20s, officials told me that nearly 10 per cent of their population is in some form of solitary confinement on any given day…
>
> One girl from Florida described to me how she coped. "Me? I cut myself. I started doing it because it is the only release of my pain. I'd see the blood and I'd be happy … I did it with staples, not razors. When I see the blood … it makes me want to keep going." (Kysel 2012)

That so many minors in solitary harm themselves is tragic—and not surprising given the grim conditions and total isolation.

2.3 Overview of Issues

On any given day, approximately 80,000 prisoners are being held in solitary confinement in the United States alone. That's not all. According to the Bureau of Justice Statistics, over the course of a year, nearly 1 in 5 (=20%) U.S. prisoners spent time in solitary confinement, which means incarceration plus solitary confinement is imposed on approximately 400,000 people each year (Ahalt and Williams 2016). With such staggering numbers, a lot more needs to be done to justify this practice.

Others convey similar sentiments and raise important concerns. For instance, it's not only prisoners who are subjected to solitary confinement. Immigrants in detention facilities and minors in juvenile detention are also at risk.

John V. Kelly, then-US Department of Homeland Security Acting Inspector General pointed out that, "Staff did not always treat detainees respectfully and professionally, and some facilities may have misused segregation" (Sacchetti 2017). He cited the case of a detainee being locked down for multiple days for sharing coffee with another detainee (Office of Inspector General, Homeland Security 2017). This is clearly an overreaction to a minor offense.

2.4 The Harms of Solitary

Misuse is one concern. So are the extreme conditions and the resulting psychological effects. Craig Haney undertook a 2-year study of inmates who were subjected to prolonged solitary confinement at Pelican Bay prison in California. He says that,

> Sealed for years in a hermetic environment—one inmate likened the prison's solitary confinement unit to "a weapons lab or a place for human experiments"— prisoners recounted struggling daily to maintain their sanity.
>
> They spoke of longing to catch sight of a tree or a bird. Many responded to their isolation by shutting down their emotions and withdrawing even further, shunning even the meager human conversation and company they were afforded. (Goode 2015)

Haney said that, after months or years of complete isolation, many prisoners begin to lose the ability to initiate behavior of any kind. In extreme cases, "prisoners may literally stop behaving," thus becoming "essentially catatonic" (Gawande 2009).

In addition, almost 90 per cent of these prisoners had difficulties with "irrational anger," as Terry Anderson noted about his own experience. In contrast, only three per cent of the general population are said to suffer extreme anger. Not surprising, Haney claims that many prisoners in solitary become consumed with revenge fantasies.

This is a far cry from the rehabilitation that Quakers sought in turning to solitary confinement. Rather than a time to cool off, solitary seems more likely to bring emotions to the boiling point. Just look at some of the harms that have been documented.

Atul Gawande (2009) reports that studies show diffuse slowing of brain waves after a week or more of solitary confinement. He cites the 1992 case of fifty-seven prisoners of war whose EEGs showed brain abnormalities months after a 6-month detention in Yugoslavia. Such evidence indicates solitary confinement has both physical as well as psychological harms.

2.5 Abusive and Aggressive Forms of Solitary

If things aren't bad enough when people are confined to eight-by-ten-foot cells, there have been even more alarming cases. A macabre turn of events has been the use of boxes (for example with Abu Zubaydah and Mohammed Ahmed Mohammed al-Shoroeiya to cram suspected terrorists into) (Rosenberg 2019; Ackerman 2012). Yes, boxes. Presumably this is to encourage them to be more forthcoming—as if subjecting them to such miserable conditions would inspire them to divulge useful information. The result is that their confinement is more physically taxing than with the use of rooms or prison cells.

Such an extreme has been accepted if not sanctioned at the highest level. In fact, psychologist-masterminds Drs. Mitchell and Jessen recommended using such "aggressive techniques" as part of the interrogation process on so-called high-value captives. This included detainees Abu Zubaydah and Mohamed Ben Soud being placed in wooden boxes with holes poked in them to allow air flow (Fink and Risen 2017). They were then forced into crouched positions, unable to stand up or move about. The Senate Intelligence Committee Report details Zubaydah's confinement to a box:

> He spent a total of 266 hours (11 days, two hours) in the large (coffin size) confinement box and 29 hours in a small confinement box, which had a width of 21 inches, a depth of 2.5 feet, and a height of 2.5 feet... According to the daily cables... Abu frequently "cried," "begged," "pleaded," and "whimpered," but continued to deny that he had any additional information. (2014, pp. 52–53)

To add to the pressure, then US District Attorney Jay Bybee authorized via a memo the use of insects placed in the box to exploit the victim's phobias and fears. The memo permitted Zubaydah to be kept in a dark, confined space small enough to restrict his movement (CNN 2009).

> In addition, putting a [so-called] harmless insect into the box with Zubaydah, who "appears to have a fear of insects," and telling him it is a stinging insect would be allowed, as long as Zubaydah was informed the insect's sting would not be fatal or cause severe pain. "If, however, you were to place the insect in the box without informing him that you are doing so … you should not affirmatively lead him to believe that any insect is present which has a sting that could produce severe pain or suffering or even cause his death," the memo said. (CNN 2009)

2.6 Descriptions and Denials

The six cases of solitary confinement are disturbing enough when looking at the individuals affected, not to mention those like Abu Zubaydah and Ben Soud, who were crammed into boxes. It is also important to consider the scope of the use of solitary and how it can be obscured or hidden by the way it is described. We see this in the following mixture of linguistic manipulation and denial:

> "The Bureau [of Prisons] does not recognize the term solitary confinement. Therefore, the Bureau does not have a definition or reference to provide," the BOP told investigators with the DOJ [Department of Justice] Office of the Inspector General.
>
> One former BOP official told investigators that "solitary confinement does not exist" within the federal prisons system. But the inspector general's office said the Bureau of Prisons is just arguing semantics. (Reilly 2017)

Moreover, as law professor Joseph Margulies points out, there is no upper bound on holding a detainee in solitary confinement or being subjected to interrogations (2006, p. 107). To get a sense of the enormity of the problem in the US, look at the numbers reported in May, 2023 by the US Department of Justice on the Federal Bureau of Prisons:

> About 122,840 people in federal and state adult prisons and federal and local jails were placed in restrictive housing—informally known as solitary confinement—for 22 hours or more on a given day in mid-2019, according to a 2023 report released by the federal Bureau of Justice Statistics (BJS) as well as by state prison systems.
>
> That amounts to about 6% of the total U.S. prison and jail population at the time. (Ortiz 2023)

2.7 The Use of Euphemisms

One of the ways that solitary confinement has been made more palatable was through distorting language. Whitewashing it with euphemisms like "disciplinary segregation," "administrative segregation" or "Segregated Housing Units (SHU)" does not alter the fact that such isolation is harmful and its extensive use alarming. With such labeling, they can avoid admitting that they practice solitary confinement. To what advantage? Humanities professor emerita Colin Dayan asserts, "Since prison officials claim that these units are non-punitive, they are difficult to fight" (2007, p. 54).

The Washington Post Editorial Board (2017) responded to the Department of Justice report by declaring solitary confinement to be torture. "Restrictive housing placement is the bureau's preferred terminology," they stated, "but the report released last week made clear that is a semantic dodge." *The Post* pointed out that:

> Among those forced to languish alone were inmates with serious mental illness, some of whom were isolated for more than five years. A number of state prison systems have taken steps to limit or end their use of solitary confinement because of mounting evidence of its detrimental effects.
>
> The Inspector General cited research that isolation can cause anxiety, depression, anger, paranoia and psychosis among prisoners. "You have no contact, you don't speak to anybody, and it's a form of torture on some level," a psychologist at one prison told investigators.

2.8 Where Is the Outrage?

Given this is the case, it is puzzling how little outcry there is among medical personnel and the general public. The solution? *The Post* calls it:

> Ending such barbarity is not only morally correct but also has practical benefits in improving public safety. Prisoners subjected to solitary confinement have difficulty reentering society and are more likely to re-offend. (2017)

Colin Dayan observes that solitary confinement was once considered the most severe deprivation and now its use is normalized (2007, p. 54). However, change is finally afoot. We see this in the practice of solitary confinement being banned in the state of Colorado. Rick Raemisch, the Executive Director of the Colorado Department of Corrections, explained:

> Long-term solitary was supposed to be rehabilitative, but it did not have that effect. Studies have found that inmates who have spent time in solitary confinement are more likely to reoffend than those who have not. Data shows that prisoners in solitary account for about half of all prison suicides; self-harm is also more common in solitary units than in less-restrictive ones. (Raemicsh 2017)
>
> A February 15, 2024 report of the Department of Justice Office of the Inspector General documented that nearly half of all deaths by suicide in federal Bureau of Prisons custody (46 percent) take place in solitary. (U.S. Department of Justice Office of the Inspector General 2024)
>
> One social psychologist even found that the degree of loneliness experienced by people in solitary is matched only by that of terminal cancer patients. In addition, solitary confinement was intended to be a last resort for those who were too violent to be in a prison's general population. But then we gradually included inmates who disrupted the efficient

> running of an institution. In other words, inmates could be placed in solitary for almost any reason, and they were. (Raemisch 2017)

2.9 Working for Change

Raemisch came to see that major changes were in order. He noted how he benefited from listening to the perspectives of others. This came about in 2015 when he assisted the State Department with other United Nations countries in modernizing international standards for the treatment of prisoners—known as the Nelson Mandela Rules (see Chap. 14). It was decided, Raemisch (2017) reports, that keeping someone for more than fifteen days in solitary was torture.

This conclusion was echoed in a report of the Human Rights Clinic at the University of Texas School of Law. "Its authors concluded," reports Jacey Fortin, "that solitary confinement in Texas violates international human rights standards and amounts to a form of torture" (2017). The bottom line is that:

> We agree that if somebody commits a crime, they should receive a punishment… But we say, at the same time, that once you impose a punishment on a person, you need to keep treating that person with humanity and with dignity. (Fortin 2017)

Raemisch would concur. As he puts it, "There now is enough data to convince me that long-term isolation manufactures and aggravates mental illness. It has not solved any problems; at best it has maintained them. That's why, in September, Colorado ended the practice" (2017).

This decision is significant; others should follow their example. We need to recognize that its widespread use in the U. S. doesn't make it right. Many other countries are in the same boat in the use and misuse of solitary.

> In an October17, 2016 [meeting] UN Special Rapporteur on Torture, Juan E. Méndez, presented a report to the General Assembly detailing and comparing solitary confinement practices around the world. He declared that solitary confinement may amount to cruel, inhuman, or degrading treatment and in some cases torture, and may thus, under certain conditions, be prohibited under international law.
>
> In that 2011 report, Méndez further called for a categorical ban on subjecting juveniles and people with mental illness to solitary confinement, and to end the practice of prolonged and indefinite solitary confinement. (Solitary Watch 2016)

In contrast, Norway is at the other end of the spectrum in its use of solitary confinement. As Ahalt and Williams (2016) indicate, Norwegian leaders realized that the old model simply did not work—that it did more harm than good and the time had come for its replacement. Norway's approach stands as a dramatic contrast with the systemic overuse of solitary.

2.10 What Role Can Doctors Play?

Doctors have a role to play in this. The Norwegian model is worth serious consideration. Ahalt and Williams (2016) offer their recommendation—one it behooves health professionals to take. "We believe the health professions have a responsibility to work with criminal justice policymakers to assess the risk of health-related harm underlying correctional practices such as solitary confinement. Fortunately, a compelling model for such a partnership exists." This they saw practiced at a Norwegian maximum-security prison. It housed 250 men, many serving long sentences for violent crimes.

> We asked the warden how many prisoners were being held in isolation and were surprised to hear his answer: one. That morning, a prisoner had trashed his cell. Guards, using motivational interviewing strategies, tried unsuccessfully to defuse the situation. The man was now cooling off in isolation under the close supervision of a health care team. "As soon as he calms down," the warden told us, "He will return to the general population." We asked how long that might take. "Tonight?" the warden guessed. "Tomorrow, certainly." (Ahalt and Williams 2016)

In comparison:

> In a U.S. prison of the same size, we would expect to find 25 prisoners in solitary, and roughly half of them would be confined for more than a month. But here there was only one serving less than 1 day, with enhanced attention rather than minimal human contact.
>
> The Norwegian criminal justice leaders we spoke with told us that 20 years ago their correctional system resembled ours: overcrowded and violent, with frequent use of solitary confinement. Then, motivated by prison riots, Norwegian leaders undertook broad reform. (Ahalt and Williams 2016)

Norway is not alone casting a critical eye on solitary in trying to make changes with this outdated and harmful model. What is going on in Britain also deserves our attention. Jean Casella (2015) of Solitary Watch reports on controls that have been put in place:

> Britain has a long history of using solitary confinement. In 1842, it mimicked the United States in opening a prison, … devoted to isolating prisoners so they could contemplate their sins. The practice was largely abandoned on both sides of the Atlantic once it became clear that solitary led to madness, not penitence. Prison isolation was revived in the late 20th Century, but never on the scale seen in the United States. …
>
> Today, a series of rules allow the short-term use of solitary confinement, but are meant to check its overuse and abuse. Prison governors (wardens) may place individuals in what are officially called "care and separation" units to preserve the "good order and discipline" of the prison. But after 72 hours, their continued segregation requires the approval of not only the governor, but—as confirmed in a recent court decision—the Cabinet Secretary for Justice. With the necessary approvals, terms in solitary can stretch longer, but must be reviewed and renewed every 14 days.

With the additional oversight and a high-level approvals process, the abuse of solitary confinement should be curtailed. Moreover, this model allows for more transparency and thus has less likelihood of misuse.

2.11 Conclusion

There is little doubt that solitary confinement is cruel and unusual punishment and, for any extended period, is a form of torture. It has no obvious value as an instrument of rehabilitation. That it has not yet been banned or subjected to strict limitations in terms of use and duration is simply deplorable.

Both Norway and Britain have moved to a different model of addressing behavioral or other issues that made solitary seem a legitimate option. We need to give close attention to the approaches they have taken and consider the range of alternatives to solitary.

Although it seems unreasonable to have oversight by a governor, a director of justice or the like, an oversight committee could be employed to help end the abuses taking place with solitary confinement.

One option might be to use a review board such as a bioethics committee or a variation thereof, drawing upon medical professionals, clergy, and members of the community. In other words, we need more transparency about what is taking place and more controls on what is being done.

References

Ackerman, Spencer. 2012, September 8. U.S. used this torture box to interrogate Gadhafi's enemies. *Wired*. https://www.wired.com/2012/09/helping-gadhafi-torture/

Ahalt, Cyrus, and Brie Williams. 2016. Reforming Solitary-Confinement Policy — Heeding a Presidential Call to Action. *New England Journal of Medicine* 374:1704–1706. http://www.stop-solitaryforkids.org/wp-content/uploads/2016/05/NEJM-Solitary-May-2016-p1601399.pdf.

Brewster, Murray. 2018, February 8. Alleged ISIS operative 'Jihadi Jack' begs Canada to let him come here. *CBC News*. http://www.cbc.ca/news/politics/jihadi-jack-isis-consular-1.4526882

Casella, Jean. 2015. October 21. Off the block. *Solitary Watch*. http://solitarywatch.com/2015/10/21/off-the-block/.

CNN. 2009, April 17. 2002 Memo: Had to be intent to inflict 'severe pain' to b torture. CNN.

Dayan, Colin. 2007. *The story of cruel and unusual*. Boston: MIT Press.

Fink, Sheri and James Risen. 2017, June 20. Psychologists open a window on brutal C.I.A. interrogations. *The New York Times*.

Fortin, Jacey. 2017, April 26. Report compares Texas' solitary confinement policies to torture. *The New York Times*. https://www.nytimes.com/2017/04/26/us/texas-death-row-torture-report.html

Gawande, Atul. 2009, March 30. Hellhole. *The New Yorker*. https://www.newyorker.com/magazine/2009/03/30/hellhole

Goode, Erica. 2015, August 3. Solitary confinement: Punished for life. *The New York Times*. https://www.nytimes.com/2015/08/04/health/solitary-confinement-mental-illness.html

History.com. 2009, December 4. 1991: Hostage Terry Anderson freed in Lebanon. https://www.history.com/this-day-in-history/hostage-terry-anderson-freed-in-lebanon

Kennedy, Merrit. 2016, February 19. Last of 'Angola 3' released after more than 40 years in solitary confinement. *National Public Radio*. https://www.npr.org/sections/thetwo-way/2016/02/19/467406096/last-of-angola-3-released-after-more-than-40-years-in-solitary-confinement

Kysel, Ian. 2012, October 19. How not to rehabilitate young prisoners. *Al Jazeera*. https://www.aljazeera.com/opinions/2012/10/19/how-not-to-rehabilitate-young-prisoners/

Manson, Joshua. 2016, October 28. UN report compare solitary practices in the US and around the world. *Solitary Watch*. http://solitarywatch.com/2016/10/28/un-report-compares-solitary-confinement-practices-around-the-world/.
Margulies, Joseph. 2006. *Guantánamo and the abuse of presidential power*. New York: Simon & Schuster.
Office of the Inspector General. 2017, July. *Review of the Federal Bureau of Prisons' use of restrictive housing for inmates with mental illness*. US Department of Justice. https://oig.justice.gov/reports/2017/e1705.pdf#page=1.
Office of Inspector General. 2017, December 11. Concerns about ICE detainee treatment and care at detention facilities. *Homeland Security*. https://www.oig.dhs.gov/sites/default/files/assets/2017-12/OIG-18-32-Dec17.pdf.
Office of the Inspector General. 2024, February 15. *Evaluation of issues surrounding inmate deaths in Federal Bureau of Prisons Institutions*. U.S. Department of Justice https://oig.justice.gov/reports/evaluation-issues-surrounding-inmate-deaths-federal-bureau-prisons-institutions
Ortiz, Erik. 2023, May 23. New report reveals over 122K are held in solitary confinement in U.S. prisons and jails. NBC News. https://www.nbcnews.com/news/us-news/new-report-reveals-122k-are-held-solitary-confinement-us-prisons-jails-rcna84840
Pilkington, Ed. 2016, February 20. Albert Woodfox speaks after 43 years in solitary confinement: I would not let them drive me insane. *The Guardian (UK)*. https://www.theguardian.com/us-news/2016/feb/20/albert-woodfox-angola-3-first-interview-trump-confinement
Raemisch, Rick. 2017, October 12. Why we ended long-term solitary confinement in Colorado. *The New York Times*. https://www.nytimes.com/2017/10/12/opinion/solitary-confinement-colorado-prison.html
Reilly, Ryan J. 2017, July 12. Federal Prisons Officials claim inmates aren't held in solitary. DOJ Watchdog says they are. *Huffington Post*. https://www.huffingtonpost.com/entry/federal-prison-solitary-confinement-mental-illness_us_59664623e4b005b0fdca5f85?nf5.
Richey, Warren. 2007, August 13. US terror interrogation went too far, experts say. *Christian Science Monitor*. https://www.csmonitor.com/2007/0813/p01s03-usju.html
Rosenberg, Carol. 2019, December 5. What the C.I.A.'s Torture Program looked like to the tortured. *The New York Times*. https://pulitzercenter.org/stories/what-cias-torture-program-looked-tortured
Sacchetti, Maria. 2017, December 17. Watchdog report finds moldy food, mistreatment in immigrant detention centers. *The Washington Post*.
Solitary Watch. 2016, October 28. UN report compares solitary confinement practices in the U.S. and around the world.
Sontag, Deborah. 2006, December 4. Video is a window into a terror suspect's isolation. *The New York Times*. http://www.nytimes.com/2006/12/04/us/04detain.html.
Stack, Liam. 2017, March 30. 3 men on death row in Louisiana Sue over solitary confinement. *The New York Times*. https://www.nytimes.com/2017/03/30/us/3-men-on-death-row-in-louisiana-sue-over-solitary-confinement.htm.
Sudworth, John. 2017, October 25. China lawyer recounts torture under Xi's 'War On Law' BBC News, Beijing, BBC. http://www.bbc.com/news/blogs-china-blog-41661862
Teays, Wanda. 2019. Solitary confinement. In *Doctors and torture: Medicine at the crossroads*, ed. Wanda Teays. Springer Nature Switzerland AG, International Library of Ethics, Law, and the New Medicine.
U.S. Department of Justice Office of the Inspector General. 2024, February 15. Evaluation of issues surrounding inmate deaths in Federal Bureau of Prisons Institutions. Office of Inspector General DOJ. https://oig.justice.gov/reports/evaluation-issues-surrounding-inmate-deaths-federal-bureau-prisons-institutions
Washington Post Editorial Board. 2017, July 15. Solitary confinement is torture. Will the Bureau of Prisons finally stop using it? *The Washington Post*. https://www.washingtonpost.com/opinions/solitary-confinement-is-torture-will-the-bureau-of-prisons-finally-stop-using-it/2017/07/15/f719de20-68c6-11e7-8eb5-cbccc2e7bfbf_story.html?utm_term=.adc722effac4.

Chapter 3
Hoods and Sandbags

Contents

3.1 Introduction

One of the widespread practices of solitary confinement—particularly since 2001 in the "war on terror"—is the use of hoods to control prisoners and detainees. Detainees have not (yet) been charged with a crime and, unlike prisoners of war (POWs), are not protected by the Geneva Conventions. As a result, detainees have been subjected to cruel and abusive practices. This includes hooding and "enhanced interrogation" (stress positions, sleep deprivation, extremes of heat and cold, forced nudity, forced feeding, waterboarding, etc.) In this chapter I will focus on hoods as a form of solitary confinement and how concerns have been raised about torture.

Consider the April 25, 2006 decision of the Movie Picture Association of America to censor the poster advertising a documentary, "The Road to Guantánamo." The poster shows a man hanging by his handcuffed wrists, with a burlap sack over his head and a blindfold tied around the hood. The reason given for the censorship "was that the burlap bag over the guy's head was depicting *torture,* which wasn't appropriate for children to see," said Howard Cohen, co-president of Roadside Attractions, distributor of the film in North America (Kennicott 2006, my emphasis).

W. Teays, *Solitary Confinement*, Library of Public Policy and Public Administration 20, https://doi.org/10.1007/978-3-031-96566-1_3

3.2 Effects of Hooding

Putting a hood or sandbag over a person's head is a quick way to dehumanize and terrify them. As Richard Jackson says, they are now faceless (2007, p. 362). And solitary—the primary means of relating to each other has been severed. With hoods in place, they can be seen but cannot see who or what they are interacting with. This puts them at a considerable disadvantage. They are stripped of their identity—their individuality effectively erased with their heads in bags. This leaves them at the mercy of those in control, which perpetrators can use to their advantage (Teays 2019, p. 77). It is a highly effective power play.

The use of hoods is a form of solitary confinement—though one that is transitional and/or short-term. It has often been used when captives or terrorism suspects are moved to or within a detention facility or during "enhanced" interrogations. It isolates and alienates anyone unlucky enough to be subjected to its use. The practice is not just harmful for those forced to wear the hoods. It also hardens those in control; those exerting their power over the hooded other.

In *Being and Nothingness*, Jean Paul Sartre argued that sadism entails the objectification of the other. We see this with hooding. It is a sadistic and objectifying practice. We might also turn this around and note that objectifying others is sadistic. Besides the sensory deprivation, hoods strip away the uniqueness and subjectivity of the individual. Hoods and isolation are destabilizing, tearing at the person's sense of place and time, notes Deborah Sontag for *The New York Times* (2006). People who are in hoods are estranged from everyone else—alienated. In many cases they also are stripped of their clothes. This forced nudity adds another element of indignity and vulnerability, raising issues of human rights.

Scott A. Allen et al. of Physicians for Human Rights (PHR) views the purpose of hooding as creating sensory deprivation, isolation and confusion (2009). That's a key function that hoods serve. Hoods disorient the captives and put them in a state of fear as to what fate awaits them. As with the segregation of solitary confinement, this is a fate for which they cannot prepare and have no control over (Teays 2019, p. 77).

The International Red Cross points out an added use of hooding. Beyond instilling a sense of fear and disorientation hoods create a dependency on their captors (NPR 2004). If people are unable to see (and with earmuffs unable to hear and with gloves unable to touch) they cannot move about freely or easily function in their environment. Furthermore, hooding also prevents them from breathing easily. Sometimes two bags are used, further restricting breathing and making them more dependent on others.

Furthermore, hooding is often used in conjunction with physical abuse, thus increasing the anxiety as to what lies ahead. This clustering of hooding and abuse is widely practiced in detention facilities and in take-out routines. Look, for instance, at the following description by a member of the Army's 82nd Airborne Division:

> Each company goes out on a mission, and you kick the door down and catch them red handed. We caught them with RPGs [rocket propelled grenades]. So, we are going to give

> you special attention. We yank them off the truck and they hit the ground hard, maybe 5-6 feet down. We took everything and searched them. Then we toss him in the PUC [Prisoners Under Control] tent with a sandbag on his head and he is zip tied.
>
> And he is like that all day, and it is 100 degrees in that tent. Once paperwork was done we started to stress them. The five-gallon water can was full of water. We would have people hold out their arms on each side parallel to the ground. After a minute your arms get tired and shake. Then we would take some water out and douse them to get them cold. And the tent is full of dust, and they get dirty and caked with it. Then we make them do pushups and jumping jacks. At the end of a guard shift they look like zombies. (Human Rights Watch 2005)

They look like zombies? No wonder, given what they just went through. The not-quite-human Other is much less likely to elicit sympathy than individuals who can look you in the eye and convey their distress, misery, and suffering. It results in a striking breakdown of communication. Even something as simple as a conversation is unlikely in such a scenario. Any verbal interchange would consist of the one with power barking commands at the one who is powerless. They are certainly not on equal footing.

This may seem convenient for interrogations or for exercising control but is at a cost for all concerned. You cannot treat others in a degrading manner without harming them. And you cannot treat others in a degrading manner without harming your own moral fiber. It is a double whammy—eventually there are repercussions. To a considerable degree our actions define us and, so, the mistreatment of others leaves a mark which is not inconsequential.

Philosopher J. Jeremy Wisnewski and behavior scientist R. D. Emerick point out that such cruelty can lead to "force drift," where one act of abuse leads to more mistreatment. Michael Gelles, a psychologist at the Naval Criminal Investigation Service explains: "Force drift" [is] a natural inclination to uncontrolled abuse when interrogators encounter resistance (Wisnewski and Emerick 2009, p. 110).

Historian of torture, Alfred McCoy, observes that "Once the subject is disoriented, interrogators can then move on to the stage of self-inflicted pain … In this latter phase, victims are made to feel responsible for their own suffering." (Wisnewski and Emerick 2009, pp. 110–111) Mind you, this conflicts with a more humane approach. Marine Major Sherwood F. Moran advised, "Know their language, know their culture, and treat the captured enemy as a human being." (Wisnewski and Emerick 2009, p. 118) Clearly that advice is not always taken.

3.3 The Cost Is Not Insignificant

The reality is that it is easier to care about others if we are on the same level of moral status or in a guardianship role. If we cannot relate to the hooded other as a person, it is not surprising that we do not treat them humanely. And if you're the one wearing the hood, how can you be anything but terrified? All boundaries of normalcy have been left behind.

On the contrary, a caring disposition is created when we have fiduciary duties to benefit or protect others. This requires us to recognize their individual dignity. Hooding, however, locks in place a power differential between the guard and the captive that can easily turn adversarial. At that point things can escalate and the door to abuse swings wide open (Teays 2019, p. 78).

It is hard to imagine a variation of hooding that is more barbaric, but duct tape may take the prize. The FBI reported that investigators wrapped a detainee's head in duct tape because he would not stop quoting the Koran. A Pentagon review in March 2008 did not condemn that strategy. Quite the opposite: the forcible use of duct tape to silence Ali al-Marri from chanting was deemed "acceptable," as noted by journalists Mark Mazzetti and Scott Shane (2008, see also Teays 2019, p. 78).

"American Taliban" John Walker Lindh also got the duct-tape treatment after his capture in Afghanistan in fall 2001. Investigative journalist Dave Lindorff reports: Shot in the leg and badly dehydrated, Lindh was hooded and left for days with an untreated wound festering, despite doctors being readily available. He was repeatedly threatened with death, kept in an enclosed, unheated and unlit metal shipping container [with holes drilled in it for air] and removed only during interrogations (Lindorff 2004).

Los Angeles Times reporter Richard Serrano points out that: "An untold number of U.S. military service members took 'souvenir' photographs' with Lindh." Aboard the ship, he was kept in irons, blindfolded, and strapped to a gurney with duct tape—"all of which made him stand out as a valued captive for the U.S." (Serrano 2002) Lindh became "a prized deer instead of a defendant," Serrano observes (Cohen 2002).

Where is the voice of moral revulsion? Where is the public outcry? Do we have no shame? Fortunately, not all stay silent. As public health professor Jerome Amir Singh contends, "The duty of care must supersede any blanket notion of loyalty, obligation, allegiance, or patriotism that the physician may feel is owed to his or her station. This is the true ethos of service to humankind." (2007) Consequently, guards, interrogators, and health professionals should object to the use of hoods and speak out against this demeaning practice.

We see, for instance, the excesses of other "civilized" countries like England. Speaking of British torture techniques, journalist David Ignatius (2005) reports that:

> The British put hoods on their IRA prisoners, just as U.S. interrogators have done in Iraq. The British approved other, harsher methods: depriving IRA prisoners of sleep, making them lean against a wall for long periods, using "white noise" that would confuse them.

That is not all—the British resorted to instilling fear:

> The clincher for British interrogators was mock execution. The preferred method in the mid-1970s was to take hooded IRA prisoners up in helicopters over the lakes near Belfast and threaten to throw them out if they didn't talk. Sometimes, they actually were thrown out. The prisoners didn't know that the helicopter was only a few yards above the water. (Ignatius 2005)

3.4 The "Five Techniques"

In 1972, following an investigation of the treatment of prisoners in Northern Ireland, then-Prime Minister Edward Heath banned the use of hooding, white noise, sleep deprivation, food deprivation and painful stress positions—known as the "five techniques." (British Broadcasting Corporation 2011, noted in Teays 2019, pp. 59–60). He made it clear that it was time to put an end to these practices.

The "five techniques" found a modified version on the part of the U.S. For example, the Department of Defense considered the following interrogation techniques to be humane and legally permissible: "isolation for more than 5 months, sleep deprivation lasting 48 to 54 days during which interrogation took place 18 to 20 hours per day, degradation, sexual humiliation, military dogs to instill fear, and exposure to extremes of heat and cold and loud noise for long periods and combinations of these techniques" (Justo 2006, p. 1462, see also Teays 2019, Chap. 6). Unfortunately, the Department of Defense's criteria for judging this "humane" was not made public.

At the May 2004 congressional hearing over interrogation practices, Deputy Defense Secretary Paul Wolfowitz and Marine Gen. Peter Pace acknowledged that practices in dozens of Iraqi jails violated the Geneva Conventions by keeping bags over prisoners' heads for 72 hours. Wolfowitz admitted, "It would strike me as not humane." (CNN 2004) Indeed.

3.5 Abusive Techniques

In addition to being crammed into a box (see Chap. 2), detainee Abu Zubaydah was subjected to extensive waterboarding. He was strapped down to a board and a sandbag, hood, or cloth was placed over his face and water poured on it. This simulated drowning created the sensation of dying. The hood or cloth functioned as both a mask and vehicle for carrying out the waterboarding. Zubaydah was waterboarded 83 times and Khalid Sheikh Mohammed (alias KSM), another suspected high-value terrorist, was waterboarded 183 times. Not surprisingly, the practice led to accusations of torture.

Given the assessment of waterboarding by counter-terrorism specialist Malcolm Nance we should be alarmed that it was ever put to use. "When done right it is *controlled death*," he says. "It does not simulate drowning, as the lungs are actually filling with water. There is no way to simulate that. The victim is drowning." (Hounshell 2007, my emphasis) it would certainly be terrifying.

3.6 Guards' Anonymity

Another function of hoods is to ensure anonymity for the guards and interrogators, making it easier to assert dominance. It also allows them to act with impunity (NPR 2004). They can then exercise power and aggression—no need to worry about the distraction of empathy. By turning individuals into faceless objects, guards are less likely to care for them or show restraint under pressure. As with solitary confinement, too easily guards become indifferent to the harmful effects of the hoods or the suffering they cause.

> "They forced us to walk like dogs on our hands and knees," said Hiadar Sabar Abed Miktub al-Aboodi, detainee No. 13077. "And …they took us to our cells, took the mattresses out and dropped water on the floor and they made us sleep on our stomachs on the floor with the *bags on our head* and they took pictures of everything." (Higham and Stephens 2004, my emphasis)
>
> The prisoners also provided accounts of how some of the photographs were staged, including the pyramid of *hooded naked prisoners*. (Higham and Stephens 2004, my emphasis).

Masked interrogators—and doctors—are mentioned elsewhere. Khalid el-Masri is a German citizen who was a victim of mistaken identity seized by the CIA as part of "extraordinary rendition." He told of an English-speaking doctor who was *masked* when he was inspected on his arrival at the "Dark Prison" in Afghanistan, where he was detained and tortured for 5 months before being released (Grey 2006, p. 88, my emphasis). Such incidents conjure up images of hooded executioners or Ku Klux Klan members seeking to hide their identity as are ICE agents in 2025 wearing masks and street clothes.

An appalling reality was CIA's detention site in Afghanistan known as COBALT (aka the Salt Pit) where detainee al-Najjar was kept hooded, isolated, and naked in total darkness. As reported by the Senate Intelligence Committee, "everything [was] done [in] silence and in the dark" (2014, p. 66). Given his mistreatment, CIA interrogators described al-Najjar as a broken man "on the verge of a complete breakdown" as a result of the isolation (Senate Intelligence Committee 2014, p. 60). How the CIA sanctioned such cruelty is hard to fathom.

The hoods may protect the guards' anonymity, but they dehumanize the subjects targeted for the displacement of rage and racist fury. With hoods in place and the other's gaze shielded, it is easier to stand on the necks and bodies of the detainees, stack them up like pieces of wood, put them in humiliating positions, rape or sodomize them, subject them to sleep deprivation, threaten to drown or electrocute them and so on. There is a reason the hooded detainee standing on a box with electrodes attached to his extended arms became an icon of horror.

That members of Congress agreed to censor the videos of Abu Ghraib speaks volumes. They refused to share what they found so morally repugnant in the photos and videos. Photos released to the public showed only adult *male* victims of abuse. Photographs of women and children being abused, raped, and humiliated were thought to elicit more outrage and repulsion by the public. Secretary of Defense

Donald Rumsfeld said they included acts that were "blatantly sadistic" (Mitchell 2005; Teays 2008, p. 78).

Such abuse is devoid of morality, like the random violence of a mob spun out of control. Just look at the photos that were made public—the ghoulish grins of pleasure, the viciousness that was unleashed, and the gleefulness in treating the "enemy" with such brutality. As "Sergeant A" of the 82nd Airborne admitted, "Some days we would just get bored so we would ...make them get in a pyramid." Moreover, "We did that for amusement" (Teays 2008, pp. 78–79).

The Department of Defense CID report reveals that others who found abuse and torture a source of entertainment. It is hard not to label this "sadistic." For example, in section 1A of Abu Ghraib there are tack marks on the wooden wall to indicate the number of stitches detainees received after being abused, particularly by dog bites. And note the grinning faces in the photographs from Abu Ghraib released in 2003. Human rights activist Susan Sontag addresses the abusive actions at Abu Ghraib and elsewhere as torture. She says,

> All the covenants on torture specify that it includes treatment intended to humiliate the victim, like leaving prisoners naked in cells and corridors. ... the horror of what is shown in the photographs cannot be separated from the horror that the photographs were taken—with the perpetrators posing, gloating, over their helpless captives...
>
> Looking at these photographs, you ask yourself, how can someone grin at the sufferings and humiliation of another human being? Set guard dogs at the genitals and legs of cowering. Naked prisoners? Force shackled, hooded prisoners to masturbate or simulate oral sex with one another? (S. Sontag 2004).

Philosopher Slavoj Zizek (2008) echoes the same concerns:

> American soldiers focused on psychological humiliation. Recording the humiliation with a camera, with the perpetrators, a stupid grin on their faces, included in the picture, side-by-side with the twisted naked bodies of their prisoners, is an integral part of the process, ... When I saw the well-known photo of a naked prisoner with a black hood covering his head, electric cables attached to his limbs, standing on a chair in a ridiculous theatrical pose, my first reaction was that this was a shot from the latest performance-art show in Lower Manhattan.
>
> To anyone acquainted with the reality of the American way of life, the photos immediately evoked the obscene underside of US popular culture—say, the initiation rituals of torture and humiliation one has to undergo in order to be accepted into a closed community. (Zizek 2008, pp. 172–173).

3.7 Patterns of Abuse

Political science professor Darius Rejali asserts that hoods were used in Brazilian and South African torture—infamous for human rights violations (Rejali 2004, Teays 2008, p. 81). Rev. George Wauchope, a torture victim under South African apartheid, pointed out that, "The use of a suffocating bag or hood around one's head, of dawn to dusk interrogation for days without a break, and of physical and psychological abuse are all forms of torture" (Wauchope 2004).

That the hooding may open the door for further abuse is truly disturbing. Some trivialize it, as with Guy Womack, attorney for M.P. reservist Charles Graner, convicted of assault and battery at Abu Ghraib. It boggles the mind that Womack could look at the piling up of hooded, naked detainees by laughing perpetrators and compare it to college sports. In his opening statement at Graner's trial, Womack said: "Don't cheerleaders all over America form pyramids six to eight times a year. Is that torture?" (Booth 2005, as noted in Teays 2008, p. 81) The barbaric nature of hoods being used today—in our names—should trouble us all. And they must cause the victims to feel that they are trapped in a horror movie.

3.8 Conclusion

Torture should be viewed as a social institution, bioethicist Steven H. Miles asserts, not a set of techniques (2006, pp. 5–6). Torturing societies create laws and policies authorizing the practices. As a result, moral responsibility must be broadly shared, rather than fall on the shoulders of a few "bad apples" (Miles 2006, pp. 5–6). We need to realize, as well, that acts of torture such as solitary confinement harm abusers as well as victims. Perpetrators cross a threshold of malice that erodes inhibitions against further acts of cruelty. Moral scars heal slowly, if at all.

As history shows, a society that sanctions or tolerates torture bears tremendous moral costs. Some believe that the utilitarian concern for society's well being overrides any prohibition against torture, as we see in "ticking bomb" scenarios. Time is running out and disaster will ensue if we do not resort to torture. That state of mind has been used to justify abusive practices around hooding and enhanced interrogation. The lack of compassion has led to considerable harm. That deserves more attention that it has received.

As philosopher Martha C. Nussbaum (2003) points out, "Compassion is not just a warm feeling in the gut, if it is that at all. It involves a set of thoughts, quite complex. Furthermore, "Compassion is an emotion directed at another person's suffering or lack of well-being. It requires the thought that the other person is in a bad way" (Nussbaum 2003, p. 234).

A central—moral—response, she argues, is to "recognize that all humans have dignity, and that dignity is both inalienable and equal, not affected by differences of class, caste, wealth, honor, status, or even sex." It enjoins us to refrain from aggression and from fraud," Nussbaum asserts (2003, p. 238).

It also enjoins us to refrain from abusive practices like solitary confinement that can have lasting harm—both physical and psychological. As we have seen from this chapter, the use of hoods is a form of solitary confinement—though one that is transitional and/or short-term. It has often been used in dealing with terrorism suspects to use hoods when captives are being moved to or within a detention facility or preceding or during "enhanced" interrogations. It isolates and alienates anyone unlucky enough to be subjected to its use. The practice is not just harmful for those forced to wear the hoods. It is also morally detrimental to those who are in control—the ones whose compassion is found lacking.

The cruelty involved in subjecting another person to hooding cannot be erased. Abu Ghraib whistleblower Joseph Darby put it this way, "it catches up to you later, when you get home. Like, I slept fine while I was there, but now I have nightmares" (Hylton 2006).

References

Allen, Scott A. 2009, August 1. Aiding Torture: Health Professionals' Ethics and Human Rights Violations. Revealed in the May 2004 CIA Inspector General's Report. *Physicians for Human Rights*. https://phr.org/our-work/resources/aiding-torture-health-professionals-ethics-and-human-rights-violations-demonstrated-in-the-may-2004-cia-inspector-generals-report/

Booth, Jenny. 2005, January 10. Torture? Not if cheerleaders do it, lawyer claims. *Bellaciao*. https://bellaciao.org/en/Iraq-torture-Not-if-cheerleaders-do-it-lawyer-claims

British Broadcasting Corporation. 2011, September 8. Baha Mousa Inquiry: 'Serious discipline breach' by Army. *BBC.com*. http://www.bbc.com/news/uk-14825889.

CNN. 2004, May 13. Pentagon leaders pressed on interrogation techniques. *CNN*. https://edition.cnn.com/2004/ALLPOLITICS/05/13/abuse.interrogation/index.html

Cohen, Andrew. 2002, April 12. Photos complicate Lindh prosecution. *CBS News*. www.cbsnews.com/stories/2002/03/21/news/opinion/courtwatch/main504297.shtml

Grey, Stephen. 2006. *Ghost plane: The true story of the CIA Torture Program*. New York: St. Martin's Press.

Higham, Scott, and Joe Stephens. 2004, May 21. New details of prison abuse emerge, Abu Ghraib detainees' statements describe sexual humiliation and savage beatings. *Washington Post*. https://www.washingtonpost.com/archive/politics/2004/05/21/new-details-of-prison-abuse-emerge/7346e4cb-47f8-42ab-8897-38a021a1bd0c/. See also, "Finding #22," Army Regulation 15-6: "Final Report. Investigation into FBI allegations of Detainee Abuse at Guantánamo Bay, Cuba Detention Facility," *Defense Link: Military News*. www.defenselink.mil/news, July 2005.

Hounshell, Blake. 2007, October 30. Ace interrogator: "Waterboarding is Torture… Period". *Foreign Policy*. https://foreignpolicy.com/2007/10/30/ace-interrogator-waterboarding-is-torture-period/

Human Rights Watch. 2005, September 22. Leadership failure: Firsthand accounts of torture of Iraqi detainees by the U.S. Army's 82nd Airborne Division. *Human Rights Watch* 17(3G). www.hrw.org/reports/2005/us0905/

Hylton, Wil S. 2006, July 31. Prisoner of conscience. GQ. https://www.gq.com/story/joe-darby-abu-ghraib

Ignatius, David. 2005, December 16. Stepping back from torture. *The Washington Post*. http://www.washingtonpost.com/wp-dyn/content/article/2005/12/15/AR2005121501438_Comments.html.

Jackson, Richard. 2007, July. Language, policy and the construction of a torture culture in the war on terrorism. *Review of International Studies 33*(3): 353-371. https://www.cambridge.org/core/journals/review-of-international-studies/article/language-policy-and-the-construction-of-a-torture-culture-in-the-war-on-terrorism/5006D871A4E5550BE5EBA0F10CCEDACF.

Justo, Luis. 2006, June 24. Doctors, interrogation, and torture. *British Medical Journal 332*(7556): 1462–1463. http://www.jstor.org/stable/25689660

Kennicott, Philip. 2006. MPAA Rates Poster an F. *Washington Post*. https://www.washingtonpost.com/archive/lifestyle/2006/05/17/mpaa-rates-poster-an-f-span-classbankheaddocumentary-

ads-image-of-guantanamo-prisoner-abuse-deemed-inappropriatespan/5f08a8ff-b09a-4e-6e-a948-3320ef41d038/
Lindorff, Dave. 2004, June 5. John Walker Lindt, Revisited. *Counterpunch*. https://www.counterpunch.org/2004/06/05/john-walker-lindh-revisited/
Mazzetti, Mark, and Scott Shane. 2008, March 13. Pentagon cites tapes showing interrogations. *The New York Times*. https://www.nytimes.com/2008/03/13/washington/13intel.html
Miles, Steven H. 2006. *Oath betrayed: Torture, medical complicity, and the war on terror*. New York: Random House.
Mitchell, Greg. 2005, September 29. Judge orders release of Abu Ghraib photos. *Editor and Publisher*. www.editorandpublisher.com/eandp/news/article_display.jsp?vnu_content_id=1001218842.
NPR. 2004, February 4. *Alleged methods of ill treatment, an excerpt from the [international] Red Cross Report on Prisoner Abuse in Iraq*. National Public Radio (NPR).
Nussbaum, Martha C. 2003. Compassion and Terror. In *Terrorism and international justice*, ed. James P. Sterba, 229–252. New York: Oxford University Press.
Rejali, Darius. 2004, April 30. Forced to stand: An expert torture. *Internationalist*. www.internationalist.org/abughraib&scigreene.html
Senate Select Committee on Intelligence. 2014, December. *The Senate Intelligence Committee on Torture*. Brooklyn: Melville House Publishing.
Serrano, Richard A. 2002, June 1. Photos of Lindh ordered destroyed. *Los Angeles Times*.
Singh, Jerome Amir. 2007, December 1. Treating war detainees and terror suspects: Legal and ethical responsibilities of military physicians. *Military Medicine*. https://academic.oup.com/milmed/article-abstract/172/suppl_2/15/4578173?redirectedFrom=fulltext&login=false#google_vignette
Sontag, Susan. 2004, May 23. Regarding the torture of others. *New York Times* magazine. https://www.nytimes.com/2004/05/23/magazine/regarding-the-torture-of-others.html
Sontag, Deborah. 2006, December 4. Video is a window into terror suspect's isolation. *New York Times*. http://www.nytimes.com/2006/12/04/us/04detain.html
Teays, Wanda. 2008. Torture and public health. In *International health policy and ethics*, ed. Michael Boylan. Springer Link.
Teays, Wanda. 2019. *Doctors and torture: Medicine at the crossroads*. Springer Nature.
Wauchope, George. 2004, June 30. Torture and politics in South Africa and Iraq. *Witness Magazine*, www.thewitness.org/printArticle.php?id=52
Wisnewski, Jeremy J., and R. D. Emerick. 2009. *The ethics of torture*. New York: Continuum International Publishing.
Zizek, Slavoj. 2008. *Violence*. New York: Picador Publishing.

Part III
Historical Perspectives

Chapter 4
Jeremy Bentham: The Panopticon

Contents

4.1 Introduction

Of Teleological Ethicists, who prioritize end goals over principles or virtues, Jeremy Bentham stands out. He has played a key role in the theory and practice. John Stuart Mill was particularly influenced by Bentham's recommendation that ethical decisions rest on action, what we need to *do* to get the best results. His intention was to set a path to the most pleasure and the least pain for the greatest number of people.

The simplicity of the maxim—the "Principle of Utility," was and continues to be especially attractive. It affirms: "Act in such a way that it results in the most pleasure and the least pain for the greatest number of people." The theory has come to be known as Utilitarianism.

In this chapter we will look at Bentham's ethical theory and his attempts at penal reform with his "Panopticon." Let's start with his contribution to Utilitarianism.

W. Teays, *Solitary Confinement*, Library of Public Policy and Public Administration 20, https://doi.org/10.1007/978-3-031-96566-1_4

4.2 Ethical Framework

Utilitarianism emphasizes potential consequences over the means. It focuses on optimizing societal benefits and minimizing harms and disadvantages. How we get to where we want to be and achieve our goals is the pivotal concern. Utilitarianism can take one of two forms—Act Utilitarianism and Rule Utilitarianism. Act Utilitarianism is used on a case-by-case basis, seeking to maximize benefits for those directly affected by the decision. In contrast, Rule Utilitarians look at the dilemma in more general terms, treating the case as a potential precedent.

Bentham's approach sets the theory apart from both Deontological Ethics and Virtue Ethics. In that respect, he is carving out new territory in terms of the theoretical structure and influence.

Here's how: Kant's Deontological Ethics centers on moral duty and the ethical principles that should guide our decision-making. He sought to universalize moral reasoning. What stands out for Kant is what we would willingly make into a universal law. Be an ethical role model. Do what you would have everyone follow suit. Kant referred to it that principle—"Choose that act that you would have it become a universal law"—as the "Categorical Imperative."

Bentham took a different route. Instead of turning our attention to abstract principles, we should focus on potential outcomes—where we want to end up. Our greatest concern should be what needs to be done to get there, aiming for the maximum pleasure and the least pain for as many people as possible. "Ethics at large may be defined," says Bentham, "as the art of directing men's actions to the production of the greatest possible quantity of happiness, on the part of those whose interest is in view" (2003, p. 49). What follows from this, observes philosopher William Sweet, is a clear division of right and wrong. That which does not maximize the greatest happiness is, therefore, morally wrong (2001).

Bentham's main concern was the society more than particular individuals. "The interest of the community," he asserts, is "the sum of the interests of the several members who compose it" (Bentham 2003, p. 9). In other words, "A thing is said to promote the interest, or to be *for* the interest, of an individual, when it tends to add to the sum total of his pleasures: or what comes to the same thing, to diminish the sum total of his pains" (Bentham 2003, p. 9).

The aggregate interests of the community should prevail in ethical decision-making. Think about this for a minute. Bentham wanted to further societal benefits and the pleasures that would ensue. Unlike Kant, Bentham would not spend as much jtime on moral obligations and principles. However useful they might be to contemplate; they are not the driving force of Utilitarian reasoning. In pursuing his Principle of Utility, he rejected the approach of Kant and other Deontological ethicists who turned the spotlight on individual moral agents. He centered his theory on bettering the community, rather than a particular collection of individuals. In that sense, Bentham's Utilitarianism had a political slant to it, given the societal focus.

Bentham's Utilitarianism also differs from Aristotle's Virtue Ethics. Aristotle focused on what it takes to live a fulfilling life, one that is purposeful. Fulfillment, he argues, is found in the development of moral character. Be the best person we can be. Let virtues guide our reasoning. For Aristotle that can be achieved by leading a life of virtue and avoiding the extremes of deficiency and excess. Follow the middle path of the intellectual and moral virtues. Moderation is the way to go in developing our moral character says Aristotle.

Where Aristotle focused on virtues and vices, Bentham's attention was on consequences and achieving end goals. Aristotle focused on the individual moral agent and maximizing virtues and minimizing vices, Bentham focused on the society and maximizing *pleasure* and minimizing *pain* for the majority. Attend to the *collective,* even if at the detriment of specific individuals. Set personal interests aside. The result would favor neutrality and impartiality, as philosophy professor Julia Driver points out. "The right action," she says, "is understood entirely in terms of consequences produced" (2014). As a result, "Consider the good of others as well as one's own good." She observes, "When one maximizes the good, it is the good *impartially* considered. My good counts for no more than anyone else's good" (Driver 2014). Therefore, we would maximize the overall good by concentrating on the community and give credence as much to the wellbeing of others as to our own.

Taking a different approach, Aristotle would say Bentham's goal of arriving at the most pleasure is misguided. Leveling the playing field would be a bad idea. Bentham thought there were no qualitative differences between pleasures—only quantitative ones. By no means would Aristotle agree with that assessment. In fact, as Driver notes, that approach left Bentham open to several criticisms:

> First, Bentham's Hedonism was too egalitarian. Simple-minded pleasures, sensual pleasures, were just as good, at least intrinsically, than more sophisticated and complex pleasures. The pleasure of drinking a beer in front of the T.V. surely doesn't rate as highly as the pleasure one gets solving a complicated math problem, or reading a poem, or listening to Mozart. (Driver 2014)

Maybe not. However, Bentham might respond that, if the quantity of pleasures exceeds the quality, there could be a greater audience enjoying the solution to a math problem than drinking beer or watching TV.

Bentham offers this example from *The Rationale of Reward:* "Prejudice apart, the game of push-pin [a children's game like Cribbage] is of equal value with the arts and sciences of music and poetry. If the game of push-pins offers more pleasure, it is more valuable than either" (Bentham 2003, p. 94).

In all fairness to Bentham, he was trying to arrive at a way to put societal benefits first and individual pleasures lower on the scale. Philosopher John Troyer explains:

> What bothered Bentham was that "the greatest happiness of the greatest number" would favor distributions that place the majority of the population at the highest level of happiness. Bentham's worry was that a dominant majority might have the power to raise its level of happiness by treating the minority badly. (Troyer 2003, p. xii)

According to Bentham, this applies to every action. He proceeded to structure his Utilitarianism setting out basic rules and duties beyond his Principle of Utility. He emphasized three rules of ethics—*prudence* (caution), *probity* (what *not* to do), and *beneficence* (what we *should* do). Be cautious, discharge the negative, and assert the positive.

The two duties that should guide us are duty to *oneself* and duty to *others,* our neighbors. They are integral to Bentham's Utilitarianism. Maximizing pleasure requires us to attend to both duties—those toward oneself and those toward others (Bentham 2003, p. 50). In determining our duty to others, Bentham said the happiness of one's neighbour may be consulted in two ways:

1. In a negative way, by forbearing to diminish it.
2. In a positive way, by studying to increase it.

A man's duty to his neighbour is accordingly partly negative and partly positive (2003, p. 50).

That means our duty to others may involve *not* doing something; thereby withholding an action. Or it may entail a positive aspect, where we do something that helps the other person and contributes to their happiness. Shrink the negative and shore up the positive.

Bentham's rules and duties helped carve out his Utilitarianism. That said, what put him on the map and lay the groundwork of his legacy was his attempt to reshape the prison system. His vision he called "the Panopticon." It has had a long-lasting effect, as we will now examine.

4.3 The Panopticon

Long before the Quakers turned to solitary confinement to transform prisons into a place of reflection and moral reformation, Jeremy Bentham pursued his brother Samuel's bright idea. That was to envision a space—a "Panopticon"—where inmates felt they were under constant surveillance. It was to be like an all-seeing eye 24/7, from whose gaze there is no escape. It is a picture of control—maximum control.

Bentham had noble aspirations. He sought a way to address penal reform and, thereby, benefit both the individual and the society. His two-part solution was "solitary and sequestered individuals" (Bentham 2017, p. 18). The prison facility was called a "Panopticon"—pan (all), opticon (seeing)—to convey a structure where people think they are watched at all times. Create an environment where individuals are isolated and sequestered—segregated—for an indeterminate period so there is no possibility of social interaction. That was the first step.

The second step was surveillance: Once sequestered, the isolated individual would be led to think he is under constant surveillance without any respite. An omnipresent observer, such as a warden or supervisor, monitors (or is thought to be monitoring) the individual's actions (2017, pp. 12–13). Those who are to be inspected should *always* feel they are under inspection or at least standing a chance of being so.

Bentham assumed the result would be transformative. For the greatest proportion of time possible, if each sequestered person thinks he is being watched, "more strong will be the feeling that he is actually under inspection," Bentham argued (2017, pp. 12–13).

The idea was that the monitoring supervisor was "seeing without being seen." In not knowing when they were under surveillance, Bentham contended, the subjects would assume that they were *always* being watched. As philosophy professor Kevin Macnish (2011) observes, "This would encourage them to be self-disciplined and well-behaved during their incarceration." That was Bentham's intention, in any case. Such a controlling environment was thought to have the ability to reform all those held in isolation.

Over the years Bentham's vision found expression in fiction and film and in actual uses of surveillance. George Orwell's *1984* extended the Panopticon to encompass the whole of society, or at least the middle classes, notes Macnish. "As the inmates of the Panopticon were reminded of the supervisor's presence by the loudspeaker, so citizens in Orwell's vision were told repeatedly that "Big Brother is watching you" (Macnish 2011).

In sum: Bentham thought the ideal prison was one with near-constant surveillance. Short of that, we should settle for prisoners *thinking* they are always watched. Through not knowing when they were under surveillance, Bentham argued, the inmates would come to assume they were constantly under surveillance and behave accordingly. By internalizing the monitoring, sequestered individuals would adapt to the restrictions and carry out the controls. Does it "sound like a great—achievable—plan? Bentham thought so. That was in the late eighteenth century. In time that presumption would get extended to the present day with the widespread use of solitary confinement. A host of assumptions followed.

- *Deterrence*: One such assumption had to do with deterrence. As Macnish points out, (2011)
- The prospect of living in this way would also deter those who visited the prison from wanting to commit crimes. Hence the Panopticon would serve as a deterrent to the inmates from misbehaving or committing future crimes and to general society from committing crimes and finding themselves so incarcerated (2011).
- *Accountability:* Bentham threw a wider net by including the omnipresent observer (the warden) in the bargain. Professor emeritus James E. Crimmins notes that, to the seemingly "constant" but unseen surveillance of the inmates by the warden, Bentham added the observation of the warden and his subordinates by the public. Interested members of the public and members of Parliament were to be guaranteed free access to the prison, making the Panopticon subject to "the great *open committee* of the tribunal of the world" (Crimmins 2023).
- *Crime prevention.* What is also important, Bentham argues, is that as much as possible each man should actually *be* under inspection. This is the ideal of an apparent omnipresent inspector watching day in and day out. In Bentham's view, the ideal can be achieved with an architectural solution; namely, the Panopticon.

Cells shooting out from the central core (tower) of surveillance should serve the desired purpose (2017, pp. 13–14, 17).

- *Security.* The Panopticon is virtually escape-proof. Bentham points out that, "Overpowering the guard requires a union of hands, and a concert among minds. But what union, or what concert, can there be among persons, no one of whom will have set eyes on any other from the first moment of entrance?" (Bentham 2017, p. 17).
- *Moral reformation.* Isolating individuals and minimizing human contact will encourage self-reflection and contribute to behavioral modification.
- *A model for other institutions.* CCTV bears some comparison to the Panopticon, as Macnish observes: "Closed Circuit Television (CCTV) cameras offer a potentially ubiquitous gaze and a hidden, anonymous watcher akin to the Panopticon on a hitherto unimaginable scale." Furthermore, "Wireless networks transmit vast quantities of information on systems vulnerable to intercept" (2011).
- *Societal benefits.* Incarcerating criminals removes them from the community, resulting in a safer society, lowering the risks of more harm and violence.
- *A model for schools and hospitals.* Bentham assumed the effectiveness of the Panopticon could be extended to other institutions. And so, he described how it could be put in effect in schools and hospitals (2017, pp. 44–45, 48–49).

Bentham set out his "Idea of the Inspection Principle" in a letter in 1787—over 200 years ago. John Troyer said,

> The more constantly the persons to be inspected are under the eyes of the persons who of Bentham's plan should inspect them, the more perfectly will the purpose of the establishment have been attained. Ideal perfection, if that were the object, would require that each person should actually be in that predicament, during every instant of time. This being impossible, the next thing to be wished for is, that, at every instant, seeing reason to believe as much, and not being able to satisfy himself to the contrary, he should *conceive* himself to be so. (Troyer 2003, p. 5)

"It is hard to imagine the occasioning justification which would see such surveillance as a proportionate response," contends Macnish. "Even major wars do not justify the perpetual monitoring of all citizens around the clock." (2011) They have almost no interaction with another human being, other than to be led in shackles to a shower or an exercise cell once or twice a week.

As is apparent, Bentham's Inspection Principle rests on a vision of near-total surveillance. He then sets out the specifics for its use in a penitentiary, including details about its construction. First, we should note what offenses Bentham considered outside the bounds of punishment. There are four cases he rules out as meriting punishment. They are:

1. Where it is *groundless*—when there is no offense for the punishment to prevent
2. Where it is *inefficacious*—when the punishment could not have prevented the offense
3. Where it is *unprofitable*—when the effect of the punishment was too expensive or the harm it would produce would be greater than what it prevented

4. Where it is *needless*—where the offense could be prevented without punishment or at a cheaper rate (Bentham 2003, p. 27)

An example of the first case—where it is groundless—would be when the person affected gave his or her consent (Bentham 2003, p. 27). Those four cases do not call for punishment, thus being sequestered and isolated would not be justified. As for the death penalty cites Crimmins,

> Given the circumstances, Bentham believed the weight of the calculation worked against the death penalty on the grounds of deterrence, the fact that it is inequitable in its application, falling mainly on the shoulders of the poor, and because it is a form of punishment that is irremissible in the face of judicial error. (2023)

In time he rejected his earlier view that the death penalty had a few applications; viz., murder and treason. "The punishment of which the efficacy… is the greatest, is evidently that of death. In this case the efficacy of it is certain. [And] in which the name of the offender, so long as he lives, may be sufficient to keep a whole nation in a flame" (Bentham 2003, p. 43).

By 1809, notes Crimmins, Bentham abandoned the exceptions and argued that no offense warranted capital punishment (2023). He was particularly concerned that the death penalty allowed no room for error. The clincher was that there would be no going back on mistaken convictions. Certainly, there have been any number of examples where innocent people have been executed.

So, let's consider the value he sees in the Panopticon for cases where punishment *is* warranted. According to Bentham, "all punishment in itself is evil. Upon the Principle of Utility, if it ought at all to be admitted, it ought only to be admitted in as far as it promises to exclude some greater evil" (2003, p. 26).

Assuming that the omnipotent warden was always watching the inmates, Bentham expected that this "new mode of obtaining power of mind over mind, in a quantity hitherto without example" would ensure that the prisoners would modify their behaviour and work hard in order to avoid chastisement and avoid punishment (UCL 2023).

The resulting plan bears striking resemblance to the structure of contemporary Supermax prisons in which inmates are sequestered potentially for an indefinite period in solitary cells. There is one key difference from Bentham's Panopticon—namely, that Supermax prisons are not open to the public being able to examine the warden, guards, and staff. Rather, members of the public cannot generally pay a visit or tour the prison. Solitary Watch points out the following:

> Most prisons in the United States contain a solitary confinement unit, and most local jails include cells where people are held in solitary. In addition, some incarcerated people are held in isolation in special "supermax" prisons, such as California's Pelican Bay, Virginia's Red Onion, and the federal government's ADX in Florence, Colorado. At least 44 states and the federal system now have supermax prisons, which are generally composed solely of solitary confinement cells. (Solitary Watch 2024)

4.4 Structuring the Panopticon

The goal of complete isolation could be achieved with a physical structure consisting of a circular building with prisoner cells occupying the circumference and the observer-supervisor at the center. The cells are divided from one another, and the prisoners are, thereby, cut off from all communication. Partitions prevent each prisoner from viewing either other inmates or the warden. The picture is one of complete solitude.

One advantage thought to result from this plan was that the isolation of the prisoners from one another effectively prohibited escapes, since they would have no means of collusion. As Bentham put it, "no quarrelings, nor confederatings, nor plotting to escape; nor yet any whips or fetters to prevent it" (2017, p. 19). He sees the solitude to be all-encompassing: "The prisoners were to lie, as they were to eat, to work, to pray, and to do everything, in their cells, and nowhere else" (2017, p. 40). We might also note that, in addition to no possible collusion of the inmates, the physical structure of the Panopticon makes escape virtually impossible.

As we have seen with the use of solitary confinement, the consequences of isolated cells are dire and long-reaching. It is hard to imagine that Bentham pictured the harms that would be unleashed if the Panopticon system were put in place.

The ideal penitentiary, contends Bentham, would have five aspects: namely,

- Safe Custody
- Confinement
- Solitude
- Forced Labor
- Instruction

One difference in Bentham's suggested penitentiary versus current prisons is that, in his plan, there is "little ground" for subjecting offenders to solitary before conviction or restricting their communication (2017, p. 41). Until they were actually convicted individuals would not be placed in solitary confinement. Neither would they be subjected to forced labor, since he considered forced labor to be *punishment*. Therefore, those not (yet) convicted would not be subjected to such punishment.

Bentham's goal was to *internalize* the restrictions and thereby transform prisons into "penitentiary inspection-houses" (2017, p. 6). The object of the inspection principle, he asserted, "is to make them not only *suspect,* but be *assured,* that whatever they do is known, even though that should not be the case" (2017, p. 54). In this respect, Bentham thought a system of controls would be established.

4.5 Applying the Panopticon to Other Institutions

Although prisons were the focus of Bentham's Panopticon, he saw its value for four other institutions. These are asylums, hospitals, manufacturers, and schools, all of which he thought could benefit from instituting policies and practices spelled out for prisons. They would all be subject to the inspection-principle with a physical structure and use of partitions allowing the omnipresent observers (surgeons, supervisors, schoolteachers, etc.) to see without being seen. In the case of hospitals, the separation of the cells could be accomplished with curtains and shades or awnings on the windows, and short screens like the head of a cradle on the beds (Bentham 2017, pp. 45–46). Schools would be structured similarly, as Bentham explains:

> All play, all chattering—in short, all distraction of every kind, is effectively banished by the central and covered situation of the master, seconded by partitions or screens between the scholars, as slight as you please.... That species of fraud. ... called cribbing, ... will never creep in here. (Bentham 2017, p. 48)

A key factor of putting the inspection principle to work is "the inhabitants [students] being separated from one another by *partitions* but exposed alike to the view of a master at his walks, by a kind of a *grated window* in each door" (Bentham 2017, p. 49). The result in all these applications is the individuals are isolated and sequestered—confined and potentially under ongoing surveillance.

Bentham sees aspects of his Panopticon to be applicable to these other institutions, particularly in segregating and isolating inmates, patients, laborers, and students. The result, he assumes, will be better for the sequestered individuals and the society than what had been the norm.

4.6 Issues and Concerns

Bentham did not take up the mental health concerns that would result, as we have seen with the suicidal depression so many sequestered people experience. Policy analyst Andrea Fenster (2020) reports for Prison Policy Initiative:

> The new study shows that the effects of solitary confinement go well beyond the consequences identified by previous research, like anxiety, depression, and hallucinations... any amount of time spent in solitary confinement increases the risk of death in the first year after individuals return to the community, including deaths by suicide, homicide, and opioid overdose.

As noted by Solitary Watch (2024), one concern has to do with suicidal tendencies and self-harm. For example, there are alarming statistics revealing the dangers of being in solitary confinement for an extensive amount of time.

Solitary Watch (2024) points out that, in 2013, forensic psychiatrist Dr. Raymond Patterson reported that people held in California's Security Housing Units and Administrative Segregation Units had a 33 times greater chance of suicide than someone in the prison system's general population. Studies in New York and Texas also found significantly higher suicide rates in solitary.

Concerns such as suicidal depression and self-harm did not receive any attention from Bentham. He seemed either unaware of such issues or did not consider them worth mentioning. In fact, he seemed oblivious to the risks of isolating and sequestering individuals. He appears to have an overwhelmingly positive attitude about the use of his Panopticon. Given Bentham never saw it put in place, his optimism is not bolstered by evidence. Instead, he seems to assume that isolation has considerable benefits and few risks.

Bentham found it surprising that the inspection principle had not been previously considered. "My wonder," he observed, "is not only that this plan should never have hitherto been put in practice, but how any other should ever have been thought of" (2017, p. 54).

On the other hand, Bentham said, "I should suppose the inspection principle must long ago have occurred to the ingenious and have been rejected by the judicious" perhaps because of cost considerations (2017, pp. 54–55). Of course, cost is not the only factor to be considered.

4.7 Solitary Confinement

Unfortunately, Bentham did not live to see his penitentiary inspection-house made a reality in the current Supermax prisons. The question is what he would think of solitary confinement once he saw it in action. He did not appear to foresee the harmful effects it would have on someone especially for a prolonged length of time. How could he comprehend the human cost of not being able to interact with others? The social isolation would be devastating.

It is no mistake on feminist ethicist Nel Noddings' part to consider isolation a manifestation of evil, as we will see in Chap. 12. The utter cruelty of confining another person to a cell, cage, or box and having all communication cut off boggles the mind. That it can go on for years or even decades is unimaginable.

It should be recognized that one way solitary confinement was made more palatable was through distorting language with the use of euphemisms. Replacing "solitary confinement" with such terms as "disciplinary segregation," "administrative segregation," "Restrictive Housing Unit" (RHU), "Diversionary Treatment Unit" (DTU), or "Segregated Housing Unit" (SHU) does not alter the reality of what the individual is subjected to. Psychiatrist Terry Kupers refers to these as "isolation units," because "their primary purpose is to use isolation and sensory deprivation as tools of punishment" (Hattery and Smith 2023, p. 23).

> Whatever you call it, the fact is that the person is put in a small cell in isolation, with no meaningful contact with another human being. As one prisoner said, "I'm being treated like an animal. I feel lost and forgotten." And, in a very real sense, they *are* "lost and forgotten." (Hattery and Smith 2023, p. 23)

With such non-punitive labeling, institutions can avoid acknowledging that they are using solitary confinement. Such slippery use of language is difficult to fight, as law professor Colin Dayan points out (2007, p. 54). *The Washington Post* Editorial Board (2017) considers the use of such euphemisms to be a "semantic dodge." In any case, however many semantic dodges are employed, they cannot escape the fact that the conditions are extreme and the harms significant. It is not surprising that those in such extreme isolation should feel "lost and forgotten." In a very real sense, they are.

4.8 Conclusion

The fantasy of the Quakers who thought solitary confinement would purify the soul and be an effective form of rehabilitation has been shown to be groundless. That it has continued to the present day and is commonly used on both adults and juveniles shows how problematic and ill-advised is this policy and how urgent is the need to put an end to it. In the chapters that follow, we will see what the major ethicists and contemporary philosophers would think of the practice.

Ironically enough, voters in California took a stand against confining (sequestering) chickens and pigs so any movement would be impossible. Consumers and animal rights activists wanted free range—happy—chickens and pigs that could have enough space to turn around. The 2023 law—Proposition 12–in California, requires breeding pigs to be confined to a pen with no less than 24 square feet of floor space, allowing them to fully move about in their living area (Goldberg 2023).

Furthermore, as of January 2015, all of California's 15 million egg-laying hens were freed from the cramped, restrictive battery cages that had long been used on most egg farms. They now have enough space to stand up, lie down, turn around, and spread their wings without touching another bird (*L.A. Times* Editorial Board 2014).

Think about these changes regarding the treatment of animals. Surely, we could extend such freedom of movement to humans. It would seem to follow that one of our next steps would be to address the inhuman conditions used on people.

Mind you, although solitary confinement is more narrowly targeted—in prisons, jails, detention facilities and, to a lesser degree schools and hospitals—surveillance has seen widespread use, affecting most of the population. As pointed out on Criminology Web:

> Interestingly, though, some people have argued that the way in which modern technology operates is similar to Bentham's Panopticon. Public places are watched by CCTV, and so people who are in those places are seen without seeing. Similarly, people's Internet and computer usage may be watched without them being able to see whether or not they're being watched. So, in a sense, Bentham's Panopticon may have become a reality, even when the prison that he designed was never built.

References

Bentham, Jeremy. 2017. *Panopticon*. Whithorn: Anodos Books.

Criminology Web. Jeremy Bentham and the Panopticon Prison. https://criminologyweb.com/jeremy-bentham-panopticon/.

Crimmins, James E. 2023, Fall. Jeremy Bentham. In *The Stanford encyclopedia of philosophy*, ed. Edward N. Zalta and Uri Nodelman. (Fall 2023 Edition). https://plato.stanford.edu/archives/fall2023/entries/bentham/

Dayan, Colin. 2014. *The story of cruel and unusual*. Boston: MIT Press.

Driver, Julia. 2014. The history of utilitarianism. In *The Stanford encyclopedia of philosophy*, ed. Edward N. Zalta and Uri Nodelman. (Winter 2022 Edition). https://plato.stanford.edu/entries/utilitarianism-history/.

Editorial Board, *Los Angeles Times*. 2014, December 26. Editorial: California's egg-laying hens to get their breathing room. *The Los Angeles Times*.

Fenster, Andrea. 2020, October 13. New data: Solitary confinement increases risk of premature death after release. Prison Policy Initiative. https://www.prisonpolicy.org/blog/2020/10/13/solitary_mortality_risk/

Goldberg, Noah. 2023, July 3. Anti-cruelty law that gives pigs more space could raise ham, bacon prices. *The Los Angeles Times*.

Hattery, Angela J., and Earl Smith. 2023. *Way down in the hole*. Camden New Brunswick: Rutgers University Press.

Macnish, Kevin. 2011. Surveillance ethics. *Internet Encyclopedia of Philosophy*. https://iep.utm.edu/surv-eth/

Solitary Watch. 2024. Solitary confinement in the United States: The facts. *Solitary Watch*. https://solitarywatch.org/facts/faq/

Sudworth, John. 2017, October 25. China Lawyer recounts torture under Xi's 'War on Law'. BBC News, Beijing, BBC. http://www.bbc.com/news/blogs-china-blog-41661862

Sweet, William. 2001. Jeremy Bentham (1748—1832). *Internet encyclopedia of philosophy*. https://iep.utm.edu/jeremy-bentham/

Troyer, John. 2003. Introduction. In *The classic utilitarians: Bentham and Mill*. Indianapolis: Hackett Publishing.

UCL. 2023. *Panopticon. Bentham Project*. University College London. https://www.ucl.ac.uk/bentham-project/who-was-jeremy-bentham/panopticon.

Washington Post Editorial Board. 2017, July 15. Solitary confinement is torture. Will the bureau of prisons finally stop using it? *The Washington Post*. https://www.washingtonpost.com/opinions/solitary-confinement-is-torture-will-the-bureau-of-prisons-finally-stop-using-it/2017/07/15/f719de20-68c6-11e7-8eb5-cbccc2e7bfbf_story.html?utm_term=.adc722effac4.

Chapter 5
John Stuart Mill: On Societal Benefits

Contents

5.1 Introduction

If we want a theoretical framework that emphasizes end goals, Teleological Ethics is the way to go. Its focus is on consequences, rather than means or abstract principles. It shifts the spotlight from the individual to the society, seeking to maximize benefits and minimize harms for the greatest number of people. The superstar of Teleological Ethics is John Stuart Mill, who, along with Jeremy Bentham, laid the foundation of Utilitarianism. "No person is an entirely isolated being," Mill observes (2003a, p. 212). We are members of a community, and its betterment merits our utmost concern. In this chapter we will get an overview of Mill's Utilitarianism and its application to solitary confinement.

If Mill was transported into the present, he would be alarmed at the widespread use of solitary confinement. "Something is wrong with this picture," he would say. The "solitary" in "solitary confinement" is an affront to human nature. The practice does not maximize happiness or social benefits. The segregation, isolation, and sensory deprivation does little or no good and an awful lot of harm in most uses of solitary (in contrast, for example, to holding someone in solitary to protect them).

W. Teays, *Solitary Confinement*, Library of Public Policy and Public Administration 20, https://doi.org/10.1007/978-3-031-96566-1_5

Mill points out a major concern. "Next to selfishness, the principal cause which makes life unsatisfactory is want of mental cultivation" (2003b, p. 105). Clearly there is little chance of mental cultivation when you are locked in a cell 22–24 hours a day, with virtually no human contact. Albert Woodfox, who spent 43 years in solitary said, "One of the greatest hardships for me in the first few months I was at Angola was getting used to the sameness of every day"(2019). And so, "I used to talk to myself to convince myself I was strong enough to survive, just to hold on to my sanity until the feeling went away," notes *Guardian* reporter Ed Pilkington (2016). As the following case demonstrates, it is a dire situation:

> William Blake, who spent 34 years in solitary confinement in New York before he was transferred to the general prison population in 2021, described his environment in solitary as follows: "Life in the box is about an austere sameness that makes it difficult to tell one day from a thousand others. Nothing much and nothing new ever happen to tell you if it's a Monday or a Friday, March or September, 1987 or 2012… I've seen and felt hope becoming like a foggy ephemeral thing, hard to get ahold of, even harder to keep ahold of as the years and then decades disappeared while I stayed trapped in the emptiness of the SHU [Segregated Housing Unit] world." (Solitary Watch 2024)

In this chapter we will look at Mill's Utilitarianism and its value in examining solitary confinement—being "trapped in emptiness," as Blake describes. With its emphasis on the best decisions and actions, Mill's approach serves as a valuable framework for our inquiry. For that reason, Mill sought to modify Jeremy Bentham's moral principle, his "Principle of Utility," and adopt a revised form. Reflecting on Bentham's approach, Mill (1833) said,

> It is perhaps fortunate that Mr. Bentham devoted a much larger share of his time and labour to the subject of legislation, than to that of morals; for the mode in which he understood and applied the Principle of Utility appears to me far more conducive to the attainment of true and valuable results in the former, than in the latter of these two branches of inquiry.

Bentham's guideline was that we should choose that act that would result in the most pleasure and least pain for the greatest number of people. Quantity matters. Mill was not inclined to prioritize pleasure. In its place, he argued, the focus should be on social benefit and happiness. Quality is more important than quantity. "The Utilitarian 'good' is no abstract metaphysical property, such as harmony with God's will, rather it is human happiness," argues research associate Karolina Gombert. "According to Utilitarian philosophy," she adds, "governments must promote human happiness, minimizing human suffering" (2014).

If solitary confinement is not a form of punishment, Mill would wonder how people end up there in the first place. As criminology research fellow Sharon Shalev notes, "Prisons do not function in a vacuum, but are part of larger criminal justice systems, which operate within wider social, cultural, political and economic systems" (2003, p. 28). As a result, addressing the issue is to the common good.

"Prisons and jails are maybe the most change-resistant government institutions we have in this country," Solitary Watch Director Jean Casella said. "So bringing any kind of change will be a long, arduous process" (cited by journalist Erik Ortiz, 2023). Fortunately, Mill offers useful tools for our quest. Let's go there next.

5.2 Ethical Framework

Mill casts the spotlight on end goals rather than moral duty (as Kant recommends) or the development of moral character (as Aristotle recommends). Help the majority, the society as a whole, rather than a single individual. His advice—his Principle of Utility—is to "Choose that act that would result in the greatest happiness and least unhappiness for the greatest number of people." Mill argues that "I must again repeat what the assailants of Utilitarianism seldom have the justice to acknowledge, that the happiness which forms the utility and standard of what is right is not the agent's own happiness, but that of all concerned" (Mill 2003b, p. 108).

Mill makes it explicit that the focus should be on "all concerned" and not the individual. "According to Mill, conceiving oneself as a morally responsible agent does not mean to see oneself as an "I" who could have acted differently. It means to consider oneself as member of a moral community entitled to sanction the violation of justified social norms," philosophy professor Michael Schefczyk points out (2012).

What follows is that "As between his own happiness, and that of others, Utilitarianism requires him to be as strictly impartial as a disinterested and benevolent spectator" (Mill 2003b, p. 108). Direct our attention to the society. Clarify goals. Weigh pros and cons and do a cost-benefit assessment. Then settle upon a decision. Keep in mind the humanity of those affected by the decision-making process.

Mill offers this analogy to drive his point home: "Human nature is not a machine to be built after a model and set to do exactly the work prescribed for it, but a tree, which requires to grow and develop itself on all sides, according to the tendency of the inward forces which make it a living thing" (Mill 2003a, p. 196).

We might see this as an organic process, where the priority is not abstract concepts or principles but actual members of a community. We should attend to the collective and its wants and needs. "One could say: the Principle of Utility is for Mill not a *component* of morality, but instead its *basis*," notes Schefczyk (2012).

Ethicist Michael Boylan looks at the impact of Utilitarianism and points out that it is the dominant moral theory in business and politics (2000, p. 82). He notes that Utilitarianism is easy to understand and that "Most adults can apprehend and readily apply the Utilitarian slogan 'The greatest good for the greatest number.'" He goes on to argue that this would be an important advantage for any theory that aspired to be adopted by some society (2000, p. 80).

"If a society educates its population properly," Boylan contends, "people would see that their own personal interests are not as important in the general scheme of things as the good of the whole." This occurs only when we feel sympathy for the other (Boylan 2000, p. 75). That sympathy is not always forthcoming, as the conditions of those subjected to solitary confinement demonstrate. That needs to change.

A minority could be marginalized or ignored altogether unless we think that their interests should matter to the general public. In general, prisoners and detainees have not merited much concern. Consequently, those who end up in solitary tend to be held in low regard, if not contempt—their moral status aligned with marginalized others.

An example is the use of forced prison labor. Phoebe Holman reports for Solitary Watch that: "Over three-quarters of all incarcerated people are forced to work without minimum wage protections for cents an hour or not paid at all in many states. The work is mandatory, and those who refuse are subjected to punishments like solitary confinement or loss of family visits" (2024).

Mill makes it clear where his priorities lie; namely, "As the means of making the nearest approach to this ideal, would enjoin, first, the laws and social arrangements should place the happiness or… the interest of every individual as nearly as possible in harmony with the interest of the whole" (2003b, p. 108). In addition, "That education and opinion, which have so vast a power over human character, should so use that power so as to establish in the mind of every individual an indissoluble association between his own happiness and the good of the whole" (Mill 2003b, p. 108).

Mill wanted to make this much clear—he's not on the same page as Kant. He took aim at Kant's Deontology (see Chap. 6) and specifically his first maxim. In Mill's opinion Kant's Categorical Imperative—to act in such a way as to make it a universal law—falls short. He said of Kant:

> This remarkable man, whose system of thought will long remain one of the landmarks in the history of philosophical speculation, does, in the treatise in question, lay down a universal first principle as the origin and ground of moral obligation; it is this: "So act that the rule on which thou actest would admit of being adopted as a law by all rational beings." (Mill 2003b, p. 97)

However, insists Mill, the Categorical Imperative has a fatal flaw; specifically,

> But when he [Kant] begins to deduce from this precept any of the actual duties of morality, he fails, almost grotesquely, to show that there would be any contradiction, any logical (not to say, physical) impossibility, in the adoption by all rational beings of the most outrageously immoral rules of conduct. All he shows is that the consequences of their universal adoption would be such as no one would choose to incur. (Mill 2003b, p. 97)

Mill asserts that, "To give any meaning to Kant's principle, the sense put upon it must be that we ought to shape our conduct by a rule which all rational beings might adopt with benefit to their collective interest" (2003b, p. 136). Collective interest is put on the front burner, while the interests of particular individuals are of lesser concern. The quest is for the greatest social benefit bearing the optimal consequences for the majority. "In particular," contends Gombert, "the normative philosophical theory of "Utilitarianism' is useful for penology. This is because Utilitarianism combines moral and political philosophy, in that it is concerned both with defining 'the good' and establishing a basis for the role of government and thus a state's political obligations" (Gombert 2014).

We need to ask ourselves, "Does our society benefit as a whole from our policies and practices, such as that of solitary confinement?" Surely there are alternatives worth considering. A central concern is whether the thousands of people subjected to such extreme isolation have been to our collective benefit. Is our society better off with the widespread use of solitary confinement and Supermax prisons designed for long-term isolation? The evidence is to the contrary. Let us see how.

5.3 Supermax Prisons

More than 44 states have Supermax prisons—a sobering reality. Sharon Shalev observes that "Supermax prisons with their austere conditions, and their near-absolute control of prisoners are presented as one of the remedies by politicians, wanting to appear to be doing something about crime" (2003, p. 32).

Moreover, the isolation of the prisoners is matched by the isolation of the prisons themselves. "Supermax prisons are typically hidden from public view, away from main roads and public life and many are located in remote rural areas." They are closed, almost hidden places, with little external or scrutiny, as Shalev points out. Prisoners describe them as like a dungeon, a cave, or a submarine with the "claustrophobia of a tomb" (2003, pp. 106, 171).

One inmate described it as like "a space capsule where one is shot into space and left in isolation." Guards and administrators have minimal contact and maximal control over the prisoners. In addition, communication with prisoners is conducted through an intercom system. Basically, it is a grim, heartless situation, "antiseptic and sterile" (Shalev 2003, pp. 119, 133).

Mill would ask: Have we gained anything by locking people away for days, weeks, years, or decades? He would have serious doubts that any benefits either for the individual or the society exceed the costs. As Mill argues,

> To recapitulate: the idea of justice supposes two things—a rule of conduct and the sentiment which sanctions the rule. The first must be supposed common to all mankind and intended for their good. The other (the sentiment) is a desire that punishment may be suffered by those who infringe the rule. (2003b, p. 136)

It may not be possible to please everyone, but we should seek the best results for the majority. The *modus operandi* of a Utilitarian is to do a cost-benefit assessment of the ethical dilemma. Factor in the end goals as bearing the greatest weight. Lower on the scale are ethical principles, moral duties, codes, good intentions, and the means to achieve the objectives. Our rallying cry is "The greatest good for the greatest number of people."

5.4 The Harm Principle

Against the background of his Principle of Utility's focus on social benefits, Mill shines a spotlight on individual freedom. He believes that individual interests should be held sovereign, limited only by nonmaleficence. This moral principle forms the basis of his "Harm Principle" which he sets out in his book *On Liberty*. Mill asserts:

"The only purpose for which power can be rightfully exercised over any member of a civilized community, against his will, is to prevent harm to others" (2003a, p. 158). *We will return to this point in the conclusion of this chapter.*

Philosophy professor Christopher Macleod (2020) points out that "An individual's action can be legitimately encroached upon if and only if that action might harm another individual. In this sense, the principle merely states the conditions under which interference is permissible—not the conditions under which it is desirable." It is then not surprising that Mill would devote attention to justice. He argues:

> Justice is a name for certain moral requirements which, regarded collectively, stand higher in the scale of social utility, and are therefore of more paramount obligation, than any others, though particular cases may occur in which some other social duty is so important as to overrule any one of the general maxims of justice. Thus, to save a life, it may not only be allowable, but a duty to steal or take by force, the necessary food or medicine, or to kidnap and compel to officiate the only qualified medical practitioner. (Mill 2003b, pp. 144–45)

A decision might cause others to suffer, which would be acceptable if the majority came out ahead. The system may not be uniformly just or treat everyone fairly and with dignity. That some fall through the cracks is a permissible compromise for Utilitarians if the majority would benefit by the decision or action. That is questionable when the prison conditions are lacking, causing those in solitary to suffer to the degree that neither they nor the society acquire any benefits.

Karolina Gombert (2014) points out that, "Achieving criminal justice through imprisonment however does not mean that prisoners experience 'justice' in terms of good humane health, hygiene and accommodation conditions, and opportunities to obtain assistance and help with rehabilitation." Moreover, "Due to the abysmal prison conditions in many developing countries, including overcrowding, prisoner-on-prisoner violence, lack of medical care, guard abuse and corruption, imprisonment may do more harm than 'justice;' transforming the offender into the victim of the legal system" (Gombert 2014).

5.5 The Injustice of Solitary Confinement

There are a number of uses—and misuses—to which solitary confinement has been put. Researcher Joshua Manson cites examples from a United Nation's report.

> In both the U.S. immigration and detention and federal prison systems, for example, people can be held in solitary confinement for the sole reason that they will be released, removed, or transferred within 24 hours. Also under U.S. federal law, people can be held in solitary confinement if they are HIV-positive and there is "reliable evidence" that they may "pose a health risk" to others. (Manson 2016)

If the goal is the path to the best consequences when facing a decision, one thing is clear: Solitary confinement would be a poor choice, other than as a temporary measure and then only on a short-term basis. Solitary confinement may be a legitimate option to protect someone from harm, such as threats of violence on the part of other inmates. Otherwise, its use should be severely restricted.

Being confined to solitary for a prolonged period has been shown to be so detrimental both physically and psychologically that death might seem preferable. The number of those in solitary attempting suicide or being driven to the depths of despair bears that out. It is an act of complete desperation.

Surgeon and health researcher Atul Gawande reports on the case of Bobby Dellelo. Dellelo was kept in solitary confinement for 5 years at Walpole prison in Massachusetts. Here's how it affected him:

> After a few months without regular social contact... he started to lose his mind. He talked to himself. He paced back and forth compulsively, shuffling along the same six-foot path for hours on end. Soon, he was having panic attacks, screaming for help. He hallucinated that the colors on the walls were changing. He became enraged by routine noises—the sound of doors opening as the guards made their hourly checks, the sounds of inmates in nearby cells. After a year or so, he was hearing voices on the television talking directly to him. He put the television under his bed and rarely took it out again. (Gawande 2009)

You don't have to be a danger to others to end up in solitary confinement, contrary to what we might think. This is particularly disturbing given the damaging effects of being isolated for even short periods. It can cause long-lasting trauma, mental suffering, and psychological harm can heighten the risk of suicide. Social psychologist Craig Haney (2021) observes that,

> Descent into mental illness is a common risk, and so is suicide. A 2014 study of the New York City jail system showed that although only 7% of the nearly 134,000 prisoners studied had been subjected to solitary confinement, 53% of the "acts of self-harm" occurred among those who had had that experience.

In Haney's view, "Everybody in prison is treated like a throwaway person. The larger society rarely thinks about those individuals' well-being'" (as cited by O'Hara 2021).

5.6 The Prison Society

In 2012 National Public Radio (NPR) did a segment on the California Supermax prison Pelican Bay. Their description reveals how austere are the facilities. Looking at the conditions brings to mind Bentham's Panopticon, with its tightly constructed surveillance controlling the inmates. Investigative correspondent Laura Sullivan (2012) reports on the prison conditions and the utter isolation of the inmates. She notes:

- First the *architecture*: "Picture spokes on a wheel, and in the center of the spoke is a correctional officer who sits behind computers and runs the system with buttons, and he's behind glass."
- Then there are *the inmates' cells*: "Down the spokes are just cell after cell after cell, and the inmates are in these eight-by-eight-foot-long cells."

- "Grey uniformity" describes *the setting*: "It's all concrete, a stainless-steel desk and a chair, and there's very little else in these cells."
- The *isolation* is palpable: Inmates are confined 22–24 hours a day
- *Exercise*: Inmates are allowed out for an hour and a half. Afterwards, "You walk back into your cell, and that's that."
- *Meals:* "Three times a day somebody comes by and slides a food tray through the slot in the door. You don't really talk to that person. And most of the people that I spoke to … hadn't spoke to anybody outside this very narrow space in years, let alone touched anybody.
- The *utter silence* is oppressive: You will not speak with the officer or interact with anybody.
- *Lack of contact.* "You're going to pass by the other cells, but the doors are made of solid steel, and they have nickel-sized holes in them. So, you can really just maybe see the eyes or some figures behind the wall, but you're not interacting with other inmates, you're not interacting with the officers."

It is unimaginable to be confined in this way. What kind of life is this? The segregated individual is definitely "trapped in emptiness," as William Blake said. The sameness of the days would be unbearable, given it can extend for weeks, years, and decades. It is a timeless realm—one of pure misery.

Looking at the effects on the individuals placed in solitary we can see how difficult it would be. And it is not just the person stuck in solitary who suffers. The harms extend beyond the individual experiencing the segregation and sensory deprivation. One unit manager compared the interaction of the staff and prisoners to dealing with a product rather than a human being: "It's a very, very mechanical, non-human process," he said (Shalev 2003, p. 176).

The wholesale dehumanization cannot help but affect the staff and medical personnel. The agony of one individual stuck in solitary spreads to the community of which he is a part. And in the case of the thousands upon thousands of victims of this practice, there is no way the prison community can remain unscathed.

Kelsey Kauffman, a former corrections officer and researcher on prisons, looked at the dehumanization of prisoners in conjunction with the fear that staff experience. She observed," If you put yourself in a frame of mind that they're animals … it is easy to penetrate the feeling of animosity, hatred, fear. Because there is a lot of fear in guards, believe me—that fear turns into hate. And how do you deal with that fear? By making him less than you" (Shalev 2003, p. 181).

However great a distance between guards and prisoners, the consequences should not be overlooked. The guards and the rest of the staff cannot easily ignore the suffering of those held in cells, devoid of human contact. Like a tomb in which they are trapped, there are no windows allowing the sights and sounds of nature. The guards absorb the despair, the depression, the rage. And they can't brush it off as they go home to their families.

The emptiness the inmates confront is an existential state—one that becomes the reality of the prison itself. Its inhumanity affects the community of which it plays a part. Being in the presence of people suffering the conditions and consequences of this practice would bear a considerable toll on the guards and others in the prison community. And it *is* a community. Like a caged animal imploding from the despair of the situation, individuals in solitary are driven to self-destruction or violence. Guards wear Army combat uniforms, bulletproof vests, surgical gloves, and goggles, to protect themselves from the urine and feces being thrown their way (Shalev 2003, p. 141). It is a demeaning, depressing situation.

In 2011, the United Nations Special Rapporteur on torture concluded that even 15 consecutive days in solitary constitutes torture or cruel, inhuman or degrading treatment. Any longer in solitary can cause irreversible harmful psychological effects, as the Center for Constitutional Rights reports (2012). Given tens of thousands of people have been subjected to solitary confinement, such harms are an issue for all concerned. We are not talking about a handful of people.

What we can infer is that, not only does the individual suffer potentially long-term damage from solitary confinement, but the harms extend to the broader circle of the prison society. The increased risks of self-destruction do not contribute to the good or happiness for the greatest number of people. It is more like a sinkhole that swallows up everyone.

In her research on Supermax prisons, Sharon Shalev was struck by comments made by the guards (2003, pp. 234–235). Their criticism shouldn't be shrugged off as inconsequential. Here is a selection:

- "Isolation in the Supermax prisons is being used primarily for convenience, and for political play with the public, who primarily wants easy, quick answers."
- "If these prisons represent the best we can do as a society, then we are a sorry lot!"
- "How do you teach compassion by forgetting that it exists? How do you rehabilitate a man by treating him like an animal?"
- "Isolation in this form brings out the worst of the worst. This is mental cruelty. These guys are left to rot or go insane."
- "Why would you put somebody in a cell with no windows and no opportunity to see the outside world for literally years? What purpose does it fulfill? Who thought up this sadistic system?"
- "If prisons are for punishment, then so be it, but don't talk about rehabilitation. They don't rehabilitate anyone."

5.7 Solitary Confinement and Recidivism

One important issue is recidivism. When offenders subjected to solitary are released from jail or prison their rate of reoffending needs to be acknowledged and addressed. Fred Patrick, director of the Center on Sentencing and Corrections at the Vera Institute of Justice, cites the nation's, staggering rate—77% of inmates released from state prisons are arrested within 5 years (Cited by Slater 2017, p. 331).

The evidence noted by sociology and research professor Christopher Wildeman and reported by James Dean (2020) for the *Cornell* (University) *Chronicle* is that

"Being placed in solitary confinement substantially increases the risk of committing more crimes after getting released from prison and may decrease the probability of employment." What Wildeman discovered is noteworthy:

> The findings from a large body of research do indicate that restrictive housing placement may do serious psychological harm to inmates... During the time that inmates are in restrictive housing, they experience a range of problems including trouble sleeping, impaired concentration, lethargy, irrational anger, depression, hallucinations, and suicidal ideation and suicide attempts. (Dean 2020)

Furthermore, the harms do not require a lengthy period of isolation. Although many of the problems increase with time in isolation, some researchers discovered that profound psychological trauma could begin even a few days after being placed in restrictive housing (Dean 2020). As a result, mental health issues come to the forefront.

Unfortunately, the traumatic results can be long-lasting: "For many, these effects do not fully dissipate after their release from restrictive housing, leading to poor mental health months and even years into the future, as Dean notes (2020). Also, "Because poor mental health is strongly linked in the general population with poor labor market outcomes... any effects of restrictive housing placement on long-term mental health could impede prisoner reentry" (Dean 2020).

The rather startling statistics indicate that being placed in solitary confinement increased the risk of being convicted of another crime within 3 years after release by about 15%. That is a 'pretty massive' increase, Wildeman notes, considering recidivism rates are already high (as quoted by Dean 2020).

5.8 Conclusion

Speaking of *On Liberty,* Mill said:

> The object of this essay is to assert one very simple principle, as entitled to govern absolutely the dealings of society with the individual in the way of compulsion and control, whether the means used be physical force in the form of legal penalties, or the moral coercion of public opinion." (2003a, p. 158)

The only justifiable interference with someone's conduct is when it concerns other people. The bottom line for Mill is this: "Over himself, over his own body and mind, the individual is sovereign" (Mill 2003a, p. 158).

This principle has had enormous impact, as it emphasizes personal autonomy and human rights. It draws a line in the sand, setting out a limit on when restrictions are called for. It has direct application to solitary confinement. As we saw from the evidence noted previously, there is no physical or moral good coming from the practice of solitary confinement.

Furthermore, human rights considerations deserve our attention. Mill's view is that any presumed good for the individual or for the society as a whole is insufficient to justify the practice of solitary confinement. He does acknowledge that the

Harm Principle is aimed at competent adults. Children may need to be protected "against their own actions as well as against external injury" (Mill 2003a, p. 158).

Only if it is necessary to prevent harm to others or oneself should solitary confinement be considered. However, should there be potential harm to others (as in a prison setting), is there any reason for requiring the extreme isolation of solitary? Surely there are other options. Weighing the advantages against the disadvantages should be clarified at the outset. That is not to say punishment should be ruled out.

> If anyone does an act hurtful to others, there is a prima facie case for punishing him by law or, where legal penalties are not safely applicable, by general disapprobation…
>
> [Similarly,] A person may cause evil to others not only by his actions but by his inaction, and in either case he is justly accountable to them for the injury." (Mill 2003a, p. 159)

Since solitary confinement does not normally function as punishment, it should be considered only when there are no alternatives with fewer destructive consequences. It is safe to conclude that solitary confinement should be banned in all cases other than for short-term protection. Even then there are better alternatives to the extreme isolation of solitary.

References

Boylan, Michael. 2000. *Basic ethics*. Upper Saddle River: Prentice Hall.

Center for Constitutional Rights. 2012, May 31. *Solitary confinement: Torture in U.S. prisons*. Updated March 2017, Center for Constitutional Rights. https://ccrjustice.org/home/get-involved/tools-resources/fact-sheets-and-faqs/torture-use-solitary-confinement-us-prisons

Dean, James. 2020, June 16. Short stays in solitary can increase recidivism, unemployment. *Cornell Chronicle*. https://news.cornell.edu/stories/2023/03/wrinkles-time-experience-linked-heartbeat

Gawande, Atul. 2009, March 23. Hellhole. *The New Yorker.* https://www.newyorker.com/magazine/2009/03/30/hellhole

Gombert, Karolina. 2014, January 1. An 'opportunistic interpretation' of bentham's panopticon writings. *Journal of Bentham Studies,* UCL Press. https://uclpress.scienceopen.com/hosted-document?doi=10.14324/111.2045-757X.003

Holman, Phoebe. 2024, May 29. Refusing forced labor is punished a with solitary. *Solitary Watch*. https://solitarywatch.org/2024/05/29/refusing-forced-labor-in-prisons-is-punished-with-solitaryand-other-news-on-solitary-confinement-this-week/

Macleod, Christopher. 2020. John Stuart Mill. In *The Stanford encyclopedia of philosophy*, ed. Edward N. Zalta. (Summer 2020 Edition) https://plato.stanford.edu/archives/sum2020/entries/mill.

Manson, Joshua. 2016, October 28. UN report compare solitary practices in the US and around the world. *Solitary Watch.* http://solitarywatch.com/2016/10/28/un-report-compares-solitary-confinement-practices-around-the-world/

Mill, John Stuart. 1833. Remarks on Bentham's philosophy. *The collected works of John Stuart Mill, Volume X, Essays on Ethics, Religion and Society*. https://en.m.wikisource.org/wiki/Remarks_on_Bentham%27s_Philosophy

Mill, John Stuart. 2003a. On liberty. In *The classical utilitarians: Bentham and Mill*, ed. John Troyer. Indianapolis: Hackett Publishing.

Mill, John Stuart. 2003b. Utilitarianism. In *The classical utilitarians: Bentham and Mill*, ed. John Troyer. Indianapolis: Hackett Publishing.

O'Hara, Delia. 2021, April 19. Craig Haney advocates for criminal justice reform. *American Psychology Association,* apa.org. https://www.apa.org/members/content/haney-criminal-justice-reform

Ortiz, Erik. 2023, May 23. New report reveals over 122K are held in solitary confinement in U.S. prisons and jails. *NBC News*. https://www.nbcnews.com/news/us-news/new-report-reveals-122k-are-held-solitary-confinement-us-prisons-jails-rcna84840

Pilkington, Ed. 2016, February 20. Albert Woodfox speaks after 43 years in solitary confinement: I would not let them drive me insane. *The Guardian* (UK). https://www.theguardian.com/us-news/2016/feb/20/albert-woodfox-angola-3-first-interview-trump-confinement

Schefczyk, Michael. 2012. John Stuart Mill: Ethics. *Internet Encyclopedia of Philosophy*. https://iep.utm.edu/mill-eth/#H9

Shalev, Sharon. 2003. *Supermax: Controlling risk through solitary confinement*. Portland: Willan Publishing.

Slater, Dashka. 2017. North Dakota's Norway experiment. In *Dismantling mass incarceration: A handbook for change*, ed. Premal Dharia, James Forman Jr., and Maria Hawilo. New York: Farrah, Straus, and Giroux.

Solitary Watch. 2024. Solitary confinement the United States: The Facts. *Solitary Watch*. https://solitarywatch.org/facts/faq/

Sullivan, Laura. 2012, June 21. The grim realities of life in prisons. Talk of The Nation, National Public Radio. https://www.NPR.Org/2012/06/21/155513749/The-Grim-Realities-Of-Life-In-Supermax-Prisons

Woodfox, Albert. 2019. *Solitary*. New York: Grove Press.

Chapter 6
Kant: On Punishment

Contents

6.1 Introduction

Solitary confinement is a strange type of punishment—if it can be considered punishment. Other than locking the offender away, what function does it serve, what are the benefits, if any? These questions merit our attention, particularly given the high number of people affected by this practice. It calls for careful consideration, thus the focus of this chapter's inquiry.

One philosopher who is most helpful to undertake this journey is Immanuel Kant. In prioritizing obligations and moral duty, he seeks to universalize human rights. Kant has had enormous impact on the field of ethics, and so it will be instructive to apply his theory to solitary confinement. He would recommend that we think carefully about subjecting individuals to such extreme isolation in light of its harms and effects on human dignity. Is this a practice that everyone should follow? Is it worth sustaining? Let us see what path Kant would take.

W. Teays, *Solitary Confinement*, Library of Public Policy and Public Administration 20, https://doi.org/10.1007/978-3-031-96566-1_6

6.2 Ethical Framework

Kant is *Numero Uno* in Deontological Ethics. The biggest issue is what rules, principles, and duties should guide us, rather than focusing on the consequences or moral character. This is a distinctly different emphasis from the Teleological Ethics' view that the end goals should drive the decision-making and from the Virtue Ethics' view that character development is our main concern.

Like Mill and Aristotle, Kant puts a lot of emphasis on rationality. But, unlike Mill, he does not see societal benefits as the primary goal and, unlike Aristotle, his main concern is not intellectual and moral virtues. Kant contends that ethical decision-making should be guided by the answer to "What are my duties here?" "What principles should guide us?" So, for example, when assessing solitary confinement as a form of punishment, we might ask ourselves:

- "What obligations should dictate who gets placed in solitary—and for how long?"
- "How ought we determine the standards and principles that should guide us?"
- "How do we balance the competing interests, such as isolating offenders while trying to utilize behavioral modification?"
- "To what degree can we match the crime with the punishment?"
- "What is the role of retribution in how we proceed?"

Kantian ethics helps us address these issues and provides some tools of analysis. In that sense, this theory is the flip side of Teleological Ethics. The focus here is on ethical principles, not end goals. This is a distinctly different emphasis from Utilitarianism. The biggest issue for Kant is what rules and principles should guide us. Kant's approach also diverges from Aristotle's focus on moral and intellectual virtues.

Basically, Kant subscribes to the view that intentions inform actions. As a result, consequences should not determine whether the decision was good. Nor should we get stuck on the various virtues Aristotle subscribes to that build moral character.

Kant rejects the Teleological view that the right choice is the one with the best overall outcome, that the goodness of the outcome decides the rightness of action. A central focus of Mill's Utilitarianism is on the most desirable outcome and not what was done to arrive at it. Philosophy professors Robert Johnson and Adam Cureton observe that Kant denies that right-and-wrong are in some way or other functions of goodness or badness. This points to a key distinction; namely, "Kant's own views have typically been classified as Deontological precisely because they have seemed to reverse this priority and deny just what such theories assert. Rightness, on the standard reading of Kant, is not grounded in the value of outcomes or character" (Johnson and Cureton 2022). In that regard, Kant rejects the approach of both Mill and Aristotle.

For Kant, the right thing to do is rooted in ethical principle, the goodness of the act itself. Kant would recommend focusing on our moral obligations and choosing that act that we would willingly have *everyone else* follow suit. Given the harms of solitary, would we want every —or any—offender to be subjected to it? "Those who are in the system are just tired of the mass incarceration," says Rick Raemisch, Colorado's prison chief (Noted by Slater 2017, p. 336). This view is echoed by Angela Y. Davis who points out that "We take prisons for granted but are often afraid to face the realities they produce" (2003, p. 15). Prisons, argues Davis, may simply be obsolete—see her book *Are Prisons Obsolete?*

Kant's spotlight is on universalizing our decision-making—thus he would also give attention to Davis' question. Let us see what that would entail. Think of it this way: When confronted with a choice, ask neither "How can I get the best outcome and maximize societal benefits?" nor "What is the best route to developing my moral character?" Instead, ask "What are my obligations, my duties, and what principles should be my guide?" The path I take should be one I would wish for everyone else.

This value carries over to the treatment of those in solitary confinement. As criminology research fellow Sharon Shalev points out, "The social distancing between 'us' and 'them' allows prison staff to treat prisoners in a way that would've been inconceivable had they viewed them as people like themselves" (2009, p. 182). We should not overlook their human dignity.

Deontological ethicists would emphasize individual rights over societal benefits. Such rights are to be defended, even if the society might benefit more from sacrificing a minority for the good of the majority. This makes for a fundamental difference from Utilitarianism and other Teleological theories, such as Moral Relativism, which prioritizes a particular group's values. Kant argues that everyone has a right to freedom by virtue of their humanity. He claims that human rights must be held sacred however great a sacrifice those in power may have to make, as philosophy professor Luigi Caranti (2022) points out. Integral to this view, says Caranti, is that we have an innate right to freedom and equality. Personal autonomy lies at the root of that freedom.

Give no credence to the potential consequences of the diverse options. The pillars we should pay attention to are the moral duties—the principles —we hold dear and nothing else. And we need to stand firm. Our motto should be "*A rule's a rule*!" So don't think exceptions should carry any weight. "Hold firm to your convictions" Kant would recommend.

6.3 Kant's Moral Principles

If you said, "I can live with exceptions" or "I'm not bothered by a little lie or two" you would *not* get the Kantian Stamp of Approval. For Deontological Ethicists like Kant, moral duty is a beacon lighting the way in ethical decision-making. Here are his two principles:

Kant's Two Moral Principles

The Categorical Imperative

Choose that act that you would be willing to become a universal law.

⟶ *Universalize ethical decision-making.*

The Humanitarian Principle
Always treat others as an end in themselves, never merely as a means.
⟶*Treat others with respect and dignity.*

With the Categorical Imperative, Kant would have us select the choice that we believe everyone else should take. Think of ourselves as ethical role models and, therefore, choose wisely. If we would not want others to do as we do, then we should consider an alternative plan. Only if we are willing to have our decision lead the way should we continue with it.

That said, we can only hold *moral agents* responsible for their behavior. Kant does not consider minors or mentally incompetent individuals to be moral agents and, therefore, they should not be judged by this standard. This links back to Kant's emphasis on rationality—being competent to make ethical decisions. Let's see what this means and how it factors into decision-making on solitary confinement.

As noted above, Kant's system rests on his two ethical principles— "imperatives." They are called *imperatives* because they are moral commands. And they are called *categorical* imperatives because they apply across the board to all rational adults (= moral agents).

Categorical imperatives are distinct from hypothetical imperatives. An imperative is hypothetical if it rests on a contingency, like a limiting context. Categorical imperatives, in contrast, are unconditional and absolute maxims. Hypothetical imperatives are not. For example, contrast the principle "It is always wrong to cheat" with "As long as you don't get caught, go ahead and cheat on the exam," Kant would have nothing to do with hypotheticals that allow for immoral acts under certain circumstances. He advocates moral principles that extend to all without any limiting preconditions. He sees them as *absolutes.*

6.4 The Categorical Imperative

Of Kant's two principles, the Categorical Imperative is more widely cited and used as a moral template ("What if everybody did it—would I then endorse this choice?)." This is the principle that asks us to *universalize* moral decision-making. An action is justifiable only if everyone could do the same. Kant thought this would lead us to being honest, keeping our promises, and so on. If we are not willing to be an ethical role model, we are not on the right track with our decision-making according to Kant.

In his opinion autonomous moral agents do not act randomly. They give careful thought to the relevant ethical principles and select the rule that guides their behavior, as Caranti asserts (2022). In line with Kant's emphasis on individual autonomy is the role of human dignity in the Humanitarian Principle. Respecting people as ends in themselves and not only as a means underscores freedom, justice, and human rights. Fairness should guard our thinking. Critics of solitary confinement often cite cases where inmates fail to be treated with the re that we give to those not incarcerated. They have little or no moral standing and the very conditions of the isolation and segregation are abusive.

Some consider Kant's Humanitarian Principle to be a version of the Golden Rule's "Do unto others as you would have them do unto you." However, there are crucial differences. In an article in *Philosophy Now,* Paul and Ally Walker (2018) explain how these two principles differ. They note that, "Kant argued that the Golden Rule is inferior to this [the Categorical] imperative: that since the Golden Rule does not contain principles of duties to one's own moral will, nor principles of 'strict obligation to one another,' it could not be a universal law."

> As an illustration, he suggests that many might willingly forego help from others if that means they will not need to help others themselves. That is compatible with the Golden Rule; but the rule that there is no need to help others could not rationally be generalized as a universal law." (Walker and Walker 2018)

Philosopher Onora O'Neill notes the significance of the "only" in Kant's maxim that we ought not treat others as *only* means. She refers to this as the "Formula of the End in Itself." To use someone as a mere means is to involve them in an act to which they could not in principle consent to (2016, p. 412). She notes that,

> Kant states the Formula of the End in Itself as follows: Act in such a way that you always treat humanity, whether in your own person or in the person of any other, never simply as a means but always at the same time as an end. To understand this, we need to know what it is to treat a person as a means or as an end. (O'Neill 2016, p. 411)

What follows is this: "A maxim expresses a person's policy, or if he or she has no settled policy, the principle underlying the particular intention or decision on which he or she acts" (O'Neill 2016, p. 411). Using someone as a means is not in itself a problem. Kant's prohibition is to to using them *only* as a means. O'Neill offers this example:

> If I cash a check I use the teller as a means, without whom I could not lay my hands on the cash; the teller in turn uses me as a means to earn his or her living. But in this … Kant would say that though they use one another as means, they do not use one another as mere means. (2016, p. 412)

Granted, people are used all the time, as when they help us get a job or introduce us to their nice cousin we are attracted to. What Kant objects to is people being used *only* as a means, as if a link in a chain and nothing more. Such misuse of others turns them into objects to be used, not subjects deserving of respect.

One way of using others as a mere means is by deceiving them. Think, for example, of all those email and phone scams we get. They are attempts to fool us into giving up our passcodes or other personal information so we can be ripped off. There's no doubt that the intention is to trick us, entrap us, use us.

Another way we might be used as mere means is by bribes ("Admit my son to the university and I will donate $50,000 to your program"), coercion ("If you want to keep your job, you need to show more loyalty to the party") and blackmail ("Pay me $1,000 a month or I will send your wife photos of you in bed with your secretary"). Each of these cases involves using others as mere means. This, for Kant, is morally impermissible.

When it comes to solitary confinement inmates have not been shown the respect they deserve as ends in themselves. We see this with the rise of Supermax prisons. Sharon Shalev reports:

> "In 1978, the Marion prison [in Ohio] was reclassified as the Federal Bureau of Prisons' highest security prison... Across the USA, protests against prison conditions was mounting and prison unrest growing." Acts of violence followed, leading to a 24-hour 'lockdown,' in which prisoners were locked in their cells for 24 hours a day, The lockdown, Shalev notes, "is widely seen as the birth of the Supermax doctrine." (2009, pp. 20–21)

The focus, Shalev points out, "was no longer on changing the individual prisoner but on managing ever-increasing prison populations" (2009, pp. 21–22). Prisoners were not seen as ends in themselves deserving respect; their humanity under the spotlight but were means to an orderly and secure institution. Supermax prisons, "designed for long-term isolation, were the proposed solution…[and] began mushrooming across the USA" (2009, p. 22).

6.5 Human Rights

Both the Categorical Imperative and the Humanitarian Principle are powerful maxims. They put human rights on center stage. If we think in terms of universalizing our ethical decision-making, the result would be to instill moral equality for all. This would effectively put an end to discriminatory thinking and prejudicial policies. Institutions would, thereby, be transformed. For example, racism in prison and jails would need to be addressed, as would the disproportionate numbers of Blacks, Latinos, and Native Americans placed in solitary. Such prejudicial treatment should not be tolerated.

If we follow the guidelines of the Humanitarian Principle, people would not be exploited or misused. Prejudicial acts and policies would have to be brought to an end. The payoff from putting these two imperatives to work would be significant.

Kant's account of human dignity is like that of the Universal Declaration, notes litigator and legal philosopher Rachel Bayefsky (2013, p. 811). It sets out fundamental human rights to be universally protected. Among those rights is "No one shall be subjected to arbitrary arrest, detention or exile" (UN 2023).

Kant's notion of dignity, Bayefsky argues, is usually characterized in terms of autonomy. To treat people with dignity, she notes, is to treat them as autonomous individuals. Base respect for persons in terms of their autonomy, not their social standing (Bayefsky 2013, pp. 811–812; see also Chap. 10). This underscores the importance of moral worth and equality.

To summarize: "A human being alone, and with him every rational creature, is an end in itself: by virtue of the autonomy of his freedom he is the subject of the moral law…. to be used never merely as a means but as at the same time an end," says Kant in his *Critique of Practical Reasoning* (as noted by Bayefsky 2013, p. 816). People have dignity, Kant asserts, because of their autonomy and that requires them to be treated as ends in themselves. With that in mind, let us look at Kant's approach to moral agency.

6.6 Moral Agency

For Kant, human dignity is identified with the capacity for rationality and personal autonomy. Moral agents must be be competent and have free will. If they lack either rationality or volition, they cannot function as moral agents. That means they should be able to act freely, not under force or coercion. All those having these two characteristics should have equal moral status.

We can only hold moral agents—not children or incompetent adults— responsible for their behavior. This links back to Kant's emphasis on personal autonomy and rationality, so we should see where it takes him.

As moral agents, we are considered rational and able to act on our own volition unless proven otherwise; so, under no coercion. As a result, we are the authors of our own punishments and rewards, philosopher Arthur Shuster argues. "If, for example, I assault someone, both the victim's injuries and my subsequent punishment can be imputed to me as their author" (2011, p. 431). Assigning responsibility then follows. Shuster notes that,

> Treating someone as an end means acting toward him in such a way that our actions can be compatible with his choices and with his ends, regardless of the content of those ends. In other words, to treat men as ends is to respect their autonomous choices, regardless of whether their ends happen happen to be harmful or beneficial. (2011, p. 431)

On this basis to treat a criminal as an end involves "imputing to him, as well as carrying out, the rightful effects of his choice" Shuster asserts (2011, p. 432). This emphasizes the choices we make and the importance of assigning guilt. In this way Kant places considerable emphasis on personal autonomy. The buck stops there.

6.7 Applying the Two Imperatives

These two maxims—the Categorical Imperative and the Humanitarian Principle—are the core of Kant's ethical theory and have wide-ranging impact. Each principle acts as a rule meant to guide us. Both rest on moral integrity and are not tied to *this* place or *that* community. Think of each decision as applying to everyone in every setting. Make it universal and make human rights central to our moral reasoning.

Here is what Kant would recommend: Try to pull far enough back to think rationally about the issues and concerns. Look carefully at your intentions and what moral duties should inform your thinking. Do *not* focus on the expectations around the result of the decision or if anyone will be happy with it. Instead, follow your ethical principles, maxims, moral duties. In Kant's view, our personal response to an ethical principle or duty is irrelevant. The rule functions separately from its effects on our emotions or state of mind.

Kantian ethics is useful for reflecting on moral lessons. For example, one of the duties that Kant emphasizes is honesty. Kant would insist on the truth, the whole truth, and nothing but. And that means no exceptions. This is a man with strong feelings about what needs to be done, and he doesn't budge. Our moral obligation is to act like an ethical role model; therefore, adhering to our principles is vital.

It may strike us as brittle as it is meant to be an unbending, exceptionless rule. Kant believes that moral duty overrides consequences; however disastrous they may be. To let the end goals drive the decision-making would be standing ethics on its head. Objectives fall behind duties as far as Kant is concerned.

Kant contends that all specific moral requirements are justified by his first maxim (Johnson and Cureton 2022). This means that immoral actions are irrational if they violate the Categorical Imperative. Rationality and free will are inextricably linked. As Johnson and Cureton explain, Kant thought conformity to the Categorical Imperative was essential to rational agency. They point out that

> This argument was based on his striking doctrine that a rational will must be regarded as autonomous, or free, in the sense of being the author of the law that binds it. The fundamental principle of morality — [the Categorical Imperative]— is none other than the law of an autonomous will … [And] it is the presence of this self-governing reason in each person that Kant thought offered decisive grounds for viewing each as possessed of equal worth and deserving of equal respect. (2022)

In discussing the use of solitary confinement in the 1800's by the Quakers, Sharon Shalev observes that they thought setting by yourself with no human contact would be transformative. They assumed that the isolation and segregation of the offenders would propel them to reflect on such ethical principles as found in the Bible. This was meant to result in the desirable moral reform and behavior modification. Shalev explains:

> In contrast to the previous forms of public and physical punishments, the new penitentiaries were centered on offenders' minds…they represented a move from body to soul in punishment, … It left the body untouched and, even better, was to be humane and carried out in private. (2009, p. 14)

And so, Shalev says, when prisoners were left alone with their conscience, guided by the prison chaplain and the good words of the Bible, they would engage in inner reflection and "contemplate their sinful past, and their more law-abiding future" (2009, p. 14). Clearly that was not in the cards.

6.8 Punishment

As philosopher Guus Duirndam (2022) points out, when we look at punishment, there are two main ways to go—focusing on the future or focusing on the past. One is to think in terms of future societal benefits; for instance, how it helps to punish offenders and deter criminals. This shines the spotlight on the future. Utilitarians take this approach in recommending the most advantageous route to bring the most happiness for the most people.

Duirndam (2022) explains: "**Forward-looking theories** try to defend the institution of punishment by appealing to its social benefits. Such theories are forward-looking because they justify punishment by pointing to the good things that will happen *after* the punishment is imposed." He notes that, "The most important social benefit of punishment is usually thought to be **deterrence…** that punishing people who have committed crimes will discourage other people from committing those crimes as well" (2022). What follows is "In this sense, punishments function a bit like **threats:** don't commit crimes, or else!" (2022).

Another social benefit of punishment is that wrongdoers will be **prevented from** committing other crimes while they are incarcerated. They cannot harm anyone outside of the prison if they are locked away. "In the case of dangerous criminals, such incapacitation provides additional societal protection" (Duindam 2022).

We might take a moment to consider the key functions of (legal) punishment. According to philosopher Zachary Hoskins they are:

1. Punishment involves the infliction of a burden.
2. Punishment is *intended* to be burdensome.
3. Punishment is imposed on someone *guilty* of an offense and as a response to that offense.
4. Punishment is meant to express condemnation, or censure, of the offense.

In other words, punishment is intended to be a penalty for someone guilty of an offense—a wrongdoer. It is the condemning element that distinguishes punishment from non-punitive penalties such as parking tickets (Feinberg 1965, pp. 398–401). Hoskins points out that the focus here is on legal punishment, not interpersonal punishment like that a parent applies to their children. He notes that,

Unlike deterrence, incapacitation does not operate by dissuading potential offenders. Incapacitation instead aims to remove dangerous people from situations in which they could commit crimes. Imprisoning someone in a solitary confinement unit, for instance, may or may not convince her not to commit crimes in the future, but while she is locked up, she will be unable to commit (most) crimes (Hoskins 2011).

In contrast, rather than being guided by the best consequences, we could focus on the offender's past actions and try to match the punishment to the crime itself. The intended goal is that the punishment should fit the crime.

As noted, we might arrive at an appropriate punishment by considering the *future* and decide accordingly. The other way is to consider the offender's behavior and factor in the actions, intentions, and duties when deciding on the punishment. The two options are to factor in the future versus to be guided by the past.

Philosopher Kevin Murtagh (2005) sums up these two approaches as follows: "Utilitarians attempt to justify punishment in terms of the balance of good over evil produced and thus focus our attention on extrinsic or consequentialist considerations." On the other hand, Retributivists like Kant seek a justification that links punishment to moral wrongdoing and, consequently, it gives offenders what they deserve. Their focus is on the intrinsic wrongfulness of the crime that merits the punishment.

Duindam offers this perspective: Kant believes punishment should never be used as a means to promote some other good for the criminal or for civil society. To emphasize potential usefulness of punishment is to fall prey to futuristic thinking—something Kant wants to avoid. He rejects forward-looking theories of punishment, which hold that promoting the good of society is the *only* purpose of punishment (Duindam 2022).

According to Kant, we should only punish someone who *deserves* to be punished and not because the society will benefit. His focus is on individual responsibility and not what might be good for the society. To prioritize the interests of the society over the individual would violate the Humanitarian Principle and is *not* the direction Kant wants us to go.

We violate a person's basic human rights if we punish them just to make the world a better place, for example with solitary confinement. Deserving the punishment is crucial to justifying its use. This raises crucial concerns regarding solitary. How can it be deserved?

To be used **merely as a means is** incompatible with the respect we are owed as human beings. This is in sync with Kant's Humanitarian Principle that we treat people as ends in themselves and never used solely for our own purposes.

Let us now consider how Kant would see whether solitary confinement would be suitable punishment for the offender's crime(s) or has another value to justify its use. To answer that, we need to examine Kant's view of retribution. So, we will start there.

6.9 Retribution

"It remains correct to look to Kant as a classic defender of retribution," points out Arthur Shuster (2011, p. 426). In particular, it is the *rationality* of retributive punishment that distinguishes it from mindless revenge (Shuster 2011, p. 427). Retribution is *not* revenge when it comes to punishment. Kant would want nothing to do with vigilantes who go outside of the system to seek revenge on an offender. He would be disgusted with all those revenge movies entertaining audiences with their mutated version of retribution and justice.

Shuster summarizes Kant's view as follows: In Kant's opinion, only retribution treats individuals as autonomous agents and as ends in themselves. Only retribution as distinguished from consequentialist punishment, "defines the imputable rightful effect of the criminal's action" by looking at the act itself and not future consequences. Consequentialist penalties have nothing to do with the criminal's choice, he contends, since they are concerned only with the future conditions, such as people's safety or societal well-being (Shuster 2011, p. 432). Retribution, in contrast, establishes a proportionality in both quantity and quality Shuster notes. The guiding principle is "like for like" or *lex talionis*—between the action (the crime) and the appropriate effect (the punishment) (2011, p. 432).

Guilt is key here. Retributivist theory, as noted earlier, contends that guilt is required for punishment, but that the appropriate type and amount of punishment is determined by the crime itself. The punishment should be an appropriate response to the crime.

In other words, Kant recognizes that "an eye for an eye" is not always possible. For example, there is no similar payback for kidnapping, carjacking, or sexual assault. In reality, it may be challenging to come up with a fitting punishment for any number of crimes. "The only just punishment with respect to the individual is one equal to the severity of the offense committed," observes Kant scholar B. Sharon Byrd. As a result, "The criminal law as directed to the court is a categorical imperative" (Byrd 1989, p. 153). Kant believes that proportionality should be factored in when we are determining punishment, however difficult that may be. Professor of philosophy and religion Peter Koritansky points out that,

> [The individual] must previously have been found *punishable* before any thought can be given to drawing from his punishment, something of use for himself or his fellow citizens. The law of punishment is a categorical imperative, and woe to him who crawls through the windings of *eudaemonism* in order to discover something that releases the criminal from punishment or even reduces its amount by the advantage it promises, in accordance with the pharisaical saying, "It is better for one man to die than for an entire people to perish."For if justice goes, there is no longer any value in human beings living on the earth ... For justice ceases to be justice if it can be bought at any price whatsoever. (2005, quoting Kant)

Philosopher Frederick Rauscher (2022) contends that issues like rehabilitation and deterrence have no role to play in assessing punishment. Those are more Utilitarian concerns, namely about future benefits. Kant is more concerned about guilt than what he would see as lesser concerns. While Kant claims that the only proper justification of punishment is guilt for a crime, he does not limit the usefulness of punishment to retributivist matters. Punishment can have as its justification only the guilt of the criminal (Rauscher 2022). One question we might ask is what *purpose* solitary confinement would serve in terms of fulfilling a role as punishment.

Kant reminds us that the Humanitarian Principle of seeing others as ends in themselves, offers guidance here. Specifically, "All other uses of punishment, such as rehabilitation (the alleged good of the criminal) or deterrence (alleged good to society) uses the criminal merely as a means" (Rauscher 2022). That is the most important thing to take away from this. "Once this guilt is determined, however, Kant does not deny that something useful can be drawn from the punishment" (Rauscher 2022).

6.10 Solitary Confinement

As we have seen Kant contends that the appropriate punishment for a crime should match as much as possible the crime itself. "Like for like." Thieves should have to pay fines. Murderers should get the death penalty. And so on. Solitary confinement would not seemingly fit as punishment if we were trying to link it to a crime, but that has not deterred anyone from its use.

It behooves us to acknowledge how widespread is the practice so we can appreciate the seriousness of its use. First, let's get an overview. Solitary Watch (2023) reports relevant facts:

- The most recent and comprehensive count found that more than 122,000 incarcerated men, women, and children were held daily in some form of isolated confinement in United States prisons and jails in 2019.
- Nearly 81,000 people—6.3 percent of the total United States prison population—were locked in solitary confinement in state or federal prison on a given day in 2019.
- An additional 42,000 people —5.5 percent of the national jail population—were locked in solitary in federal and local jails on a given day in that same year.

Second, the restrictions, as Solitary Watch observes:

- They are sent to solitary based on charges that are levied, adjudicated, and enforced by prison officials with little or no outside oversight.
- Many prison systems have a hearing process, but these are seldom more than perfunctory.
- Prison staff serve as prosecutors, judges, and juries, and there are no defense attorneys.

For example, inmates held at Pelican Bay (California) Supermax prison live in a small, cement prison cell. The facts are sobering: In 2011, 46% of those in segregated housing (solitary) at Pelican Bay had been in solitary for over 10 years.

Inside the prison are 1056 concrete cells, each about the size of a parking space, designed to reduce contact with other humans to a bare minimum. As Angela Y. Davis observes "No one— not even the most ardent defenders of the supermax—would try to argue today that absolute segregation, including sensory deprivation, is restorative and healing" (2003, p. 50).

Yen-Tung Lin and Luke Baltay (2023) report for Solitary Watch that the majority of the men were not there for acts of violence but were condemned to indefinite solitary confinement based on alleged involvement in prison gangs.

Furthermore, adults are not the only ones who land in solitary confinement. Juveniles may also be subjected to the practice. "Solitary confinement and other forms of isolation remain all too common in juvenile facilities," notes Karen Lindell, a senior attorney at the Juvenile Law Center. "As described in their report on the use of solitary confinement, almost half of juvenile facilities report using isolation to control behavior" (Dowdall et al. 2020).

At the national level, a federal law in 2016 prohibited the use of solitary confinement and involuntary seclusion to punish children — but it is only applicable to those in federal Bureau of Prison facilities. Across the country, it is up to state and local officials to regulate the use of solitary confinement.

We need to keep in mind the harms of solitary confinement. Such isolation can have an almost immediate psychological impact and cause lasting trauma in adults, research has shown, but experts say its effects on young people are more detrimental because their brains are still developing (*The Oregonian* 2020).

Looking at both adults and juveniles, the evidence is overwhelming that solitary confinement is harmful for even short periods. Kant would be particularly concerned that it does not actually function as punishment, since there is no crime that it corresponds to. If the punishment should fit the crime, what crime is solitary the punishment for? Kant would likely say, "None that I can see."

6.11 Conclusion

Kant would have nothing good to say about this practice. First, he would want to know what crimes the offenders committed, what punishment they received, and for what role solitary confinement was meant to address. He would care to find out the extent to which that punishment is considered proper retribution for their offense(s). Unless the offenders held someone hostage and in isolated quarters, there is no proportionality in quantity and quality. What crime would solitary confinement match? There is no clear retribution that would be in accordance with the principle of *lex talionis.*

As a result, Kant would look critically at the use of solitary confinement and say it fails the Humanitarian Principle by treating the offender as a mere means. There is no way that it could be made into a universal law. It is not conceivable to universalize the way these individuals are treated. Kant would contend that solitary confinement fails both of his imperatives.

First, he would not allow their treatment to become a universal law; thus violating the Categorical Imperative. In addition, it turns offenders into mere means, thus violating the Humanitarian Principle requiring others be treated as ends in themselves. Kant would also be concerned about the lack of respect shown the offenders. There is no way they are treated as ends in themselves.

Similar practices of solitary confinement have taken place on *thousands* of other inmates and for much longer periods. Many have been held for weeks, months, years, and even decades in solitary confinement. It is inconceivable that Kant would condone such treatment, even if we contorted our moral reasoning to consider it retribution.

References

Bayefsky, Rachel. 2013, December. Dignity, honour, and human rights: Kant's perspective. *Political Theory* 41(6): 809–837. https://www.law.virginia.edu/scholarship/publication/rachel-bayefsky/1276836

Byrd, B. Sharon. 1989, August. Kant's theory of punishment: Deterrence in its threat, retribution in its execution. *Law and Philosophy* 8(2): 153. https://www.ojp.gov/ncjrs/virtual-library/abstracts/kants-theory-punishment-deterrence-its-threat-retribution-its

Caranti, Luigi. 2022. Kant's social and political philosophy, Stanford Encyclopedia of Philosophy.

Davis, Angela Y. 2003. *Are prisons obsolete?* New York: Seven Stories Press.

Dowdall, Layne, Jos Fox and Chloe Johnson. 2020, August 31. *Use of solitary confinement often arbitrary and all too common*. Juvenile Law Center. https://kidsimprisoned.news21.com/solitary-confinement-kids/

Duindam, Guus. 2022. How can punishment be justified? On Kant's retributivism. In *Philosophical thought*, ed. Heather Wilburn. https://open.library.okstate.edu/introphilosophy/.

Feinberg, Joel. 1965. The expressive function of punishment. *The Monist* 49 (3): 397–423.

Hoskins, Zachary. 2011. The moral permissibility of punishment. *Internet Encyclopedia of Philosophy*. https://iep.utm.edu/m-p-puni/#H7h.

Johnson, Robert and Adam Cureton. 2022, January 21. Kant's moral philosophy. *The Stanford Encyclopedia of Philosophy*. https://plato.stanford.edu/entries/kant-moral/

Koritansky, Peter. 2005, October. Two theories of retributive punishment: Immanuel Kant and Thomas Aquinas. *History of Philosophy Quarterly* 22(4): 319. https://www.jstor.org/stable/27745035.

Lin, Yen-Tung and Luke Baltay. 2023, July 18. Gathered to mark anniversary of historic prison hunger strike, advocates vow to end solitary confinement in California. *Solitary Watch*. https://solitarywatch.org/2023/07/18/gathered-to-mark-anniversary-of-historic-prison-hunger-strike-advocates-vow-to-end-solitary-confinement-in-california/

Murtagh, Kevin. 2005. Punishment. *Internet Encyclopedia of Philosophy*. https://iep.utm.edu/punishme/

O'Neill, Onora. 2016. Originally published in 1985. A simplified account of Kant's ethics. https://users.manchester.edu/Facstaff/SSNaragon/Online/texts/201/O'Neill,%20Kant.pdf

Rauscher, Frederick. 2022, Fall. Kant's social and political philosophy. *The Stanford Encyclopedia of Philosophy* (Fall 2022 Edition). https://plato.stanford.edu/entries/kant-social-political/

Shalev, Sharon. 2009. *Supermax: Controlling risk through solitary confinement*. Portland: Willan publishing.

Shuster, Arthur. 2011. Kant on the role of the retributive outlook in moral and political life. *The Review of Politics* 73 (Summer 2011): 425–448. https://www.cambridge.org/core/journals/review-of-politics/article/abs/kant-on-the-role-of-the-retributive-outlook-in-moral-and-political-life/F8D05808CD4C15BF0A0A2A15B1ACB2C2.

Slater, Dashka. 2017. North Dakota's Norway experiment. In *Dismantling mass incarceration: A handbook for change*, ed. Premal Dharia, James Forman Jr., and Maria Hawilo. New York: Farrah, Straus, and Giroux.

Solitary Watch. 2023. For those who endure it, life in solitary confinement means living in a cell for up to 24 hours a day. Fact Sheet. *Solitary Watch*. https://solitarywatch.org/

The Oregonian. 2020, September 8. Feds ban solitary confinement for kids in prison, but state juvenile facilities still use isolation. *The Oregonian*. https://www.oregonlive.com/crime/2020/09/feds-ban-solitary-confinement-for-kids-in-prison-but-state-juvenile-facilities-still-use-isolation.html

United Nations. Universal Declaration of Human Rights. 2023. https://www.un.org/en/about-us/universal-declaration-of-human-rights

Walker, Paul, and Ally Walker. 2018, April/May. The golden rule revisited. *Philosophy Now* (125). https://philosophynow.org/issues/125/The_Golden_Rule_Revisited

Chapter 7
Aristotle: On Reformation and Rehabilitation

Contents

7.1 Introduction

In terms of influence in the field of ethics the big three are Immanuel Kant, John Stuart Mill, and Aristotle. With his focus on moral character, Aristotle takes a different approach from Deontological Ethicists like Kant and Utilitarians like Mill. His inquiry is not centered on ethical principles or consequences. In contrast to Teleological Ethics (goal-based) and Deontological Ethics (duty-based), Aristotle's Virtue Ethics' main concern is the path to a fulfilling life—one of excellence. As we

W. Teays, *Solitary Confinement*, Library of Public Policy and Public Administration 20, https://doi.org/10.1007/978-3-031-96566-1_7

will see in this chapter, Aristotle would be alarmed at the use of solitary confinement and its failure to build moral character.

There is little chance of rehabilitation or moral reformation for those isolated from human contact. Being alone for hours, days, weeks, and years on end would make developing moral virtues or achieving self-reflection difficult. One inmate who spent 25 years in solitary wrote, "As they built new walls around me it felt like I was being buried alive," notes co-director of Solitary Watch Jean Casella and journalist James Ridgeway (2017). Such long-term confinement would be a living death—like something out of a horror movie.

We will get an overview of issues and concerns regarding solitary confinement and then turn to applying Aristotle's ethical foundation.

7.2 Overview of Solitary Confinement

The number of those subjected to this practice is astounding, as every year it is in the thousands. Sociologists Angela J. Hattery and Earl Smith point out that over the course of a year approximately 20% of all prisoners and 18% of jail detainees spend time in solitary confinement. That is nearly one-fifth of all those in prisons or jails are in solitary within a year (Hattery and Smith 2023, p. 37). Let us consider how we got here. Criminology research fellow Sharon Shalev observes that,

> In the early to mid-nineteenth century, solitary confinement was the main form of imprisonment for entire prison populations, aimed at reforming convicts into law abiding citizens. By the late nineteenth century this aim was deserted, as was the practice of keeping *entire prison populations* in solitary confinement. (2009, p. 12, *my emphasis*)

As Shalev asserts, "Towards the end of the twentieth century, prolonged solitary confinement of large segments of the prison population once again returned to the fore, this time as a tool of controlling prisoners defined as 'high risk'" (Shalev 2009, p. 13).

In the federal prison system and at least 19 states corrections officials may hold people in isolation housing indefinitely (Hattery and Smith 2023, p. 38). That point needs to be emphasized: Many laws are written so prisoners could be held in solitary confinement *indefinitely*. Think of the 25 years that the "Unabomber" Ted Kaczynski spent in isolation at the ADX Supermax prison in Colorado. That he committed suicide is not surprising, particularly since he had made an earlier attempt in 1998.

> While awaiting trial, in 1998, Kaczynski attempted to hang himself with a pair of underwear. Though he was diagnosed by a psychiatrist as a paranoid schizophrenic, Kaczynski was adamant that he was not mentally ill. He eventually pleaded guilty rather than to present an insanity defense. (Associated Press 2023)

Let us consider what Aristotle would think.

7.3 Aristotle's Virtue Ethics

Aristotle believes that fulfillment comes from developing virtues and minimizing vices. His approach gives us a set of tools for developing moral reasoning and building moral character. The resulting theory is known as Virtue Ethics. It highlights the character traits necessary for becoming the best person we can be. Aristotle is the heart and soul of Virtue Ethics. He looks at rational individuals (moral agents) and asks us to examine our moral character. Put that under the spotlight. Neither consequences nor moral obligations should take priority over living a life of virtue. That is the path to finding purpose in our lives. Aristotle sets this out in his book *Nicomachean Ethics* (henceforth referred to as *NE*).

Aristotle's ethical framework enables us to see the harms and limitations that solitary confinement would pose. Those who are virtuous *show* they are good; they have excellence of character. These virtues function as ideals that help us navigate the moral terrain. They provide a framework to deal with the obstacles we face and the decisions we make.

7.4 Ethical Framework

In focusing on moral character, Aristotle takes a distinctly different approach from Deontological (duty-based) and Teleological (Consequentialist) ethicists. He is neither fixated on rules and principles nor on maximizing end goals. Aristotle's is a people-centered ethical theory. He wants us to look at the way individuals demonstrate virtue or vice by assessing how they live—their actions. Contrast his approach to that of Utilitarians like John Stuart Mill who focus on consequences and goals, not the means to those ends. A Utilitarian asks, "How can I achieve the best results for the most people? How can I maximize societal benefits?" Their eyes are on the prize, not the methods by which the prize is obtained.

And, in contrast to Deontological ethicists like Immanuel Kant, Aristotle does not ask "What duties do I have to others? What are my intentions?" He asks, "What kind of *person* do I want to become?" In rejecting both Deontological and Teleological models, his theory takes a distinctly different route. His focus is on character development.

Philosopher G.E.M. Anscombe maintains that Kantianism and Utilitarianism mistakenly placed the foundation for morality on legalistic notions such as duty and obligation. To do ethics properly, she contends, start with what it is for a human being to flourish or live well (as noted by philosophy professor emerita Marcia Homiak 2019). This is the approach that Aristotle takes.

Aristotle would not ask if we would willingly make our decisions into universal law, as Kant recommends. Developing our moral character would not be something Kant would prioritize. For Kant, moral obligation—ethical duties—should drive our decision-making, and only that. Any consequences, adverse or otherwise, should carry no influence. As a Deontologist, Kant asks, "What is your moral duty?" and tells us, "Be true to your moral obligations" even if the truth hurts or the repercussions are problematic. Try to stand up for individual rights and not lose sight of your moral duties.

Aristotle would view the focus on moral obligations to be misguided. And he would not put stock in the Utilitarian focus on end goals and prioritizing the society—the many—over the few. Aristotle would not ask, "What is your goal?" Nor would he say, "Do what you've got to do to make that happen." He believes the means matter in the quest for an objective. In Aristotle's estimation, we need to focus on moral character and examine the direction and purpose of our lives. For that reason, he highlights both intellectual and moral virtues in achieving well-being and becoming a good—virtuous—person. As we will consider shortly, solitary confinement would have no role in developing moral character.

7.5 The Significance of Practical Wisdom

Aristotle looks at the path to moral excellence and sets out the intellectual and moral qualities needed to get there. Do what we must to live with ourselves and work on our strengths and weaknesses. The goal should not be to achieve impartiality or to elevate the interests of the majority of people—the society. Rather, we should attend to the moral excellence of the individual and the steps needed to accomplish that aim.

The challenge is to steer the middle course between the extremes and do so on a habitual basis. It is not something we can grasp from a few incidents. We need to examine the totality of our actions and look for patterns of behavior. Aristotle believes that moral character is built over time. Moreover, what we *do* tells us far more about ourselves than what we say or what principles we ascribe to. Habit matters. Richard Kraut, Humanities professor and specialist in ancient Greek philosophy, explains:

> What we need, in order to live well, is a proper appreciation of the way in which such goods as friendship, pleasure, virtue, honor and wealth fit together as a whole. In order to apply that general understanding to particular cases, we must acquire, through proper upbringing and habits, the ability to see, on each occasion, which course of action is best supported by reasons. (2022)

He adds:

> Therefore, practical wisdom, as he [Aristotle] conceives it, cannot be acquired solely by learning general rules. We must also acquire, through practice, those deliberative, emotional, and social skills that enable us to put our general understanding of well-being into practice in ways that are suitable to each occasion. (2022)

Abstract principles alone do not build moral character, however useful they may be. More is required. We find that "more" in the practice, the doing. We need to pay attention to the actions, the deliberative, emotional, and social skills we develop during our lives. That's the basis of practical wisdom. Our quest starts there.

Classics scholar Edith Hall concurs: "The 'virtues' or 'routes to happiness,' are not so much qualities of character as habits that can be learned through practice" (2018, p. 100). "Yes, indeed," Aristotle would say. He emphasizes that a state of character results from the repetition of similar actions. That is what we should be looking at.

The key word here is 'repetition.' Aristotle puts it this way in being a just or temperate person: "It is correct, then, to say that a person comes to be just from doing just actions and temperate from doing temperate actions; for no one has the least prospect of becoming good from failing to do them" (*NE* 2019, p. 26). However, Aristotle points out that,

> The many, however, do not do these actions. They take refuge in arguments, thinking that they are doing philosophy, and that this is the way to become excellent people. They are like a sick person who listens attentively to the doctor, but acts on none of his instructions. Such a course of treatment will not improve the state of the sick person's body; nor will the many improve the state of their souls by this attitude to philosophy. (*NE* 2019, p. 26)

The way to become excellent, Aristotle asserts, is not through taking refuge in philosophical arguments. It is our actions that matter most. Consequently, our reasoning should be in the service of our actions.

Edith Hall points out that practical wisdom is cumulative, because perfecting the art of deliberation requires practical experience. We need to do it repeatedly and assess the results. Only then can we become competent at deliberation and able to achieve our ends (2018, pp. 64–65). Hall explains: "We deliberate *in order to act,* and that is why deliberation is prominent in the spheres of ethics and politics, which concerned with *doing* things" (2018, p. 65). "It is by a man's purposive choice that we judge his character—that is, not by *what* he does but what he does it *for,*" affirms Aristotle (as noted by Hall 2018, p. 66).

7.6 The Two Categories of Virtue

Philosopher Hilary Putnam asserts that, "Aristotle is centrally concerned with the connection between happiness and character and with the vicissitudes that can shape character" (1983, p. 197). These virtues or character traits are the key to the good life, he contends. We should direct our attention regarding character traits to two key categories—the intellectual virtues and moral virtues. Both help us develop a sense of purpose. Aristotle puts it this way:

> Virtue, then, is of two sorts, virtue of thought and virtue of character. Virtue of thought arises and grows mostly from teaching; that is why it needs experience and time. Virtue of character results from habit; hence its name 'ethical'... we acquire [virtues] just as we acquire crafts, by having first performed the actions... Similarly, then, we become just by doing just actions, temperate by doing temperate actions, brave by doing brave actions. (*NE* 2019, p. 21)

Aristotle calls the five intellectual virtues "virtue of thought." They are creativity, logical reasoning, practical wisdom, philosophical wisdom, and understanding and comprehension. He considers them the means to develop clarity of mind. This clarity of thought, rationality, is not to be minimized. More attention has been given to Aristotle's moral virtues and their role in developing moral character. That said, intellectual skills—the virtues of thought—play a role in character-building.

Aristotle's moral virtues—the virtues of character—are courage, temperance, generosity, magnificence, magnanimity, even-temperament, friendliness, honesty, wit, humility, compassionate, and righteous indignation. Our actions take place in the lives we lead, and the moral virtues are crucial in shaping our lives. Solitary confinement would develop neither the intellectual virtues nor the moral virtues. It would be unlikely for solitary confinement—particularly prolonged isolation—to help any of the virtues' development. The Quakers' experience with solitary confinement made that clear, contrary to their expectations.

Other people contribute to a richer life. We see it in our behavior and in our social connections. For instance, in discussing his concept of justice Aristotle says,

> Justice is the only virtue that seems to be another person's good, because it is related to another; for it does what benefits another, either the ruler or the fellow-member of the community. The worst person, therefore, is the one who exercises his vice towards himself and his friends as well [as towards others]. And the best person is not the one who exercises virtue [only] towards himself, but the one who [also] exercises it in relation to another, since this is a difficult task. (*NE* 2019, p. 81)

Aristotle concentrates on what it takes to achieve a life of excellence. That is why he emphasizes the intellectual and moral virtues in developing moral character and in finding a sense of purpose. Any significance placed on consequences or moral obligations should be in the service of character development. For that reason, Aristotle turns to these two types of virtues and puts them to work. Through those virtues we find the key to the good life.

7.7 Looking at Solitary

As for solitary, Aristotle would recommend a major shift in penal reform. He would say we have lost the focus in dealing with inmates, detainees, juveniles, and others. What is the goal and the effects of solitary confinement? Where is the moderation, the middle path? Why does punishment take center stage? And what form should any (desirable) punishment take? How can it lead to moral reformation and rehabilitation? Where's the proof?

Law professor Robert Condlin follows Aristotle in asserting that we learn virtues by imitating both good people and good actions. Imitation leads to integration. He says, "After a while the habit of acting in a good way becomes one's own," which law professor Lorie M. Graham affirms (1995, p. 10). It is also a source of enlightenment. When we then reflect upon the nature of the good actions we can understand the virtuous character (Graham 1995, p. 10). Being isolated and away from contact with others precludes the possibility of imitating good people or good actions. It would then be a major stumbling block in effecting change or enabling moral reformation.

7.8 Achieving Well-Being

A meaningful life, according to Aristotle, is one that results in *eudaimonia* (= contentment, well-being, flourishing). Philosopher Terence Irwin clarifies Aristotle's point: "Aristotle does not mean that we all agree that the ultimate good is a feeling of pleasure or satisfaction. He means that we agree that the ultimate good consists in the best kind of life for a human being. To achieve *eudaimonia* is to be well off over one's life as a whole" (2019, p. xvii).

Aristotle explains: "Happiness is a certain sort of activity of the soul in accord with virtue" (*NE* 2019, p. 14). To achieve such well-being, he prescribes a life of moderation. The mean at which the virtues aim, Irwin points out, is described as doing what one ought, when one ought, and so on. Aristotle remarks that it is characteristic of virtue to benefit others, and to use external goods for the common benefit of the community.

Irwin says, "The main task of political science is to select, control, and adjust the different activities and pursuits that go on in a community" (2019, p. xvii). As a result, Aristotle addresses both individuals and the communities in which they reside. In addition, states Irwin, it is reasonable for Aristotle to say that when everyone strains to do fine actions the common good is promoted (2019, pp. xxiv–xxv). We benefit as individuals and so does our community.

Irwin points out that, "The virtuous person decides on the virtuous action because it is fine; and fine action is fine because it promotes the common good…In Aristotle's view, a human being is a political animal insofar as human capacities and aims are completely fulfilled only in a community" (Irwin 2019, p. xxv).

Many character dispositions or moral traits fall along a spectrum of deficient → mean → excessive. As Aristotle puts it, "these sorts of states naturally tend to be ruined by excess and deficiency" (*NE* 2019, p. 23). His advice is for us to seek the mean. Think of a desirable moral quality. Now think of its two extremes, one with the quality in short supply and the other in excess. Neither extreme would ordinarily help cultivate moral character. Stick to the middle path.

7.9 Finding the Balance

Aristotle goes on to say that we acquire virtues as we acquire crafts, by having first performed the actions. For example, we become just by doing just actions (*NE* 2019, p. 21). This requires examining the right ways of acting; for the actions also control the sorts of states we acquire.

Those who seek a morally upstanding life, according to Aristotle, need to find the balance between passivity (weakness) and aggression (excess). That is what should be our guide. The four virtues that stand out—Aristotle's cardinal virtues—are courage, justice, wisdom, and self-control. Aristotle thinks a morally upstanding person shows the wisdom to choose carefully. With each step they should get closer to being a moral exemplar, a person others will look up to and respect.

Finding a suitable rule or ethical code to solve a moral dilemma isn't necessarily easy. As Richard Kraut says, "Living well consists in doing something, not just being in a certain state or condition" (2022). This underscores Aristotle's emphasis on habit and what we do over time to build our moral character.

7.10 The Role of Friendship

Aristotle pays a lot of attention to friendships and the role they play in our lives. Other people matter. He asserts that friendship "is most necessary for our life. For no one would choose to live without friends even if he had all the other goods" (*NE* 2019, p. 141). This is clearly an issue for those isolated by solitary confinement. Who we are—our identity—is rooted in a community. We live in a world populated by others.

Aristotle considers friendship intrinsic to happiness, to a meaningful life. Edith Hall observes that, "The effective creation of happiness, for Aristotle, cannot be achieved alone. Humans may enjoy brief periods of solitude, but they are biologically social animals. They flourish optimally when they live in association with other humans and animals and engage in reciprocal good deeds" (Hall 2018, p. 162).

This requires more than passive agreement, as Hall points out. "It is insufficient, in Virtue Ethics, merely to respond to friendly overtures: you need to be a self-starter, to initiate and actively foster cooperation yourself" (2018, p. 162). Hall also notes that, in Aristotle's political theory, "our relationships with fellow citizens are a special subcategory of utility friendship, since they exist for mutual advantage" and "city-states malfunction when there are no friendly partnerships in operation between the individuals who constitute the state" (2018, pp. 162–163).

The consequences of this view extend beyond individuals to the society as a whole. As Hall points out, "In a happy state, although citizens have different occupations, they share the common goal of their community's welfare" (2018, p. 164). A great deal follows from this. As much as the virtues lay a foundation for character development, they also lay a foundation for building a constructive community serving the well-being of its members. Such practices as solitary confinement undermine that goal by locking away—segregating—members it considers undesirable. They become outcasts.

Aristotle directs his harshest criticism at tyrannies, Hall points out, because they discourage activities that foster self-esteem and self-confidence (2018, p. 165). This criticism could also apply to Supermax prisons, with their vast exercise of control and use of prolonged isolation. There is no fostering of self-esteem or self-confidence in the way solitary confinement is practiced. Also "in a tyranny there is little or no friendship," Aristotle contends (*NE* 2019, p. 156). Clearly a black mark against tyrannies.

7.11 Solitary Confinement

Another tyrannical aspect of Supermaxes and other prisons employing long-term solitary confinement is that it can be *very* long-term. This is borne out by the 2016 United Nations report *Seeing into Solitary: A Review of the Laws and Policies of Certain Nations Regarding Solitary Confinement of Detainees*. According to the report, on any given day thousands of people around the world are subjected to some sort of solitary confinement or restricted housing. The UN report indicates that 80,000–100,000 of those held in solitary confinement around the world are incarcerated in the United States.

7.12 The Question of Benefits of Solitary Confinement

There are three major roles solitary confinement has played. They are moral reformation, behavior modification, and punishment. A less frequent use is to protect the individual. That would seem feasible only for a short period, since any long-term use of solitary confinement could lead to harms and self-destruction. Any benefits subsequent to protective isolation would cease if the isolation were extended.

That leaves moral reformation, behavioral modification, and punishment as the main goals of solitary. Each one has its limitations, as we will see. Let us start with moral reformation, as it has a long history and was born of good intentions. As we proceed, we will take note of Aristotle's likely response.

7.13 Goal #1: Moral Reformation

The first major goal of solitary confinement goes back to its original use as a tool of reflection and rehabilitation. The idea was that isolated prisoners would be compelled to reflect on their own behavior and ethical shortcomings. They would then be so thoroughly transformed that they would want no part of a life of crime. Considering the harmful consequences—the human toll—it is hard to fathom how anyone took it seriously.

The assumption was that crime bore a resemblance to a curable disease, one for which the cure was forced solitude (Shalev 2009, p. 14). The analogy between committing crimes and suffering an illness, however, falls short on several grounds. Shalev explains:

> Solitary confinement was to be the first (and essential) stage in therapeutic programmes of behaviour modification of prisoners. The logic was that an environment of unrelenting isolation would make prisoners more susceptible to the next stage of the programme: 'remoulding' through therapy and medication. (2009, p. 18)

The success of these moral reformation programs rests on the view that prisoners' minds can be turned into blank slates—a '*tabula rasa.*' Once that is accomplished, it would be possible to engrave useful traits and acceptable behavior on the mind-slate. Shalev notes that the roots of that opinion lie in John Locke's philosophy (2009, p. 19). Evidently, Locke thought a person's mind at birth was but a *tabula rasa,* upon which experience makes its imprints. If that were the case, isolating errant criminals and wiping clean their minds could lay the groundwork for moral reformation. Good luck.

Unfortunately, Locke's contention rests on a few assumptions; the foremost is that the newborn infant's mind is *actually* blank, ready for engraving. Other assumptions are that the adult mind could be erased and written upon, and that could be accomplished by the prisoner himself, once isolated from human contact. Even then, the parallel drawn between the infant's mind and that of an adult has at least one glaring difference. This is that the adult in solitary still has the use of language (that is not so easily erased). This is not the case of the newborn, who has yet to acquire linguistic tools. Can we really overlook this difference?

The long and the short of it is that attempts to reshape an individual's mind faces considerable challenges—ones not easily dismissed. The contention that long-term solitary confinement can lead to a *tabula rasa* ready for imprinting stretches reality, as the lack of evidence bears out.

There is no indication that solitary confinement has any therapeutic value. Aristotle would underscore this point. A major reason is that "The defining feature of solitary confinement, regardless of what it is officially termed, is the absolute deprivation of human interaction," stress Hattery and Smith (2023, p. 30). In working at a maximum-security prison Earl Smith discovered that prisoners serving death sentences were incarcerated in solitary confinement for the entire term of their sentences and released "only when the state deems it 'time' to take their lives" (Hattery and Smith 2023, p. 31).

This is not the situation in only one prison, as they point out. There are now hundreds of super-maximum-security "Supermax" prisons constructed entirely of units "for the long-term isolation of human beings" (Hattery and Smith 2023, p. 31). And, alarmingly enough, prisoners could be held in solitary confinement inside the United States indefinitely, as noted above (Hatterly and Smith 2023, p. 37). There is no indication of the endpoint to the confinement. That fact alone can have devastating consequences. Examples of such long-term isolation can readily be found—they are not rare occurrences. Think of mental and emotional health concerns and sell self harm.

We must ask: Can subjecting someone to solitary confinement further moral reformation? The warning signs extend back to the 1800's. Consider, for example, the observations of political theorist Alexis de Tocqueville, who came to the U.S. in

1831 to research its prison system. What he found is this: The northern wing [of the prison he examined] had eighty prisoners, each in a separate cell. He observed:

> This trial, from which so happy a result had been anticipated, was fatal to the greater part of the convicts. In order to reform them, they had been submitted to complete isolation; but this absolute solitude, if nothing interrupts it, is beyond the strength of man; it destroys the criminal without intermission and without pity; it does not reform, it kills (as quoted by Hattery and Smith 2023, p. 36).

The conclusion is a powerful indictment of the practice. Let's see how Aristotle would respond to de Tocqueville's findings. First, Aristotle would remind us that practical wisdom requires action, not just words. Ethical rules and principles may be good to consider, but they do not contribute to moral development in a vacuum. They must be set in motion through deliberate action and social skills developed in interaction with others and what we do with our values, our virtues. In looking at Aristotle's list of moral virtues, we can see that the middle path of moderation avoids the extremes of too little or too much of the character trait in question. If we demonstrate a moral deficiency, such as being apathetic on the one hand or rash or hot-headed on the other, our moral character and sense of self will suffer. It will only change if we *do* something—take action. I am defined by my deeds and the values I exhibit in living a life of purpose.

Each virtue can swing one direction or another as a result of our decision to do *this* versus *that.* Moral reformation may benefit from a short period of solitude with the time to reflect on what we are doing, how we are doing it, and what we hope to achieve. We then resume our lives in the community in which we reside. Solitary confinement has no such function or effect. The extreme isolation bears no fruit for moral reflection.

7.14 Goal #2: Rehabilitation

Closely aligned to moral reformation is rehabilitation, the second reason for adopting a policy of solitary confinement. The one—moral reformation—acts to shape or reshape the individual's value system. In this case we look at our beliefs and decide which ethical framework should be our guide. These are the duties and principles laying the foundation for engaging in moral judgments and evaluating a decision or action. Moral reformation turns a spotlight on our virtues and vices and to what degree they factor into our moral character.

Rehabilitation focuses on what we do, our actions, so we can see how to replace bad behavior with good. One way we put moral reformation to work is in our attempts at rehabilitation. This is how to put our virtues to practice, what we do to effect change and further our character development.

Considering rehabilitation as a form of behavior modification, note the comments of psychiatry and neurology specialists Hannah K. Scott et al. They observed that, "Behavior modification focuses on changing specific behaviors with little consideration of a person's thoughts or feelings." Its purpose is therapeutic; namely "to eliminate or reduce maladaptive behavior" (2023).

The ideal is to have moral reformation in sync with rehabilitation, so individuals' actions are a physical enactment of their ethics, their values. At that point we might ask: Can subjecting someone to solitary confinement further rehabilitation? Can their behavior be transformed or reshaped into actions and civility that benefit the community in a way Aristotle would applaud? That would be desirable if it could be achieved. Why isn't that possible with those in solitary confinement? Let us try to figure this out.

With the right set of virtues surely we can find the mean and live a life of purpose. And with the right sort of actions, we should be able to live peacefully in harmony with one another. Hold it right there. Live in harmony with one another? How can that aim be realized? The very reality—the fundamental reality—of solitary confinement is that the person is *confined,* locked up in the "hole"—segregated in complete isolation. There are no others to live peacefully with. Harmony is not obtainable.

There is no significant human contact beyond getting food shoved through a slot in the door or being led out for a shower or brief exercise, neither of which entail any but the most cursory interaction with other human beings. Because of this, neither moral reformation nor rehabilitation can have any chance of success. It is not foreseeable that they can make any impact whatsoever. These first two goals simply fall flat.

7.15 Goal #3: Punishment

For many people, to judge by the collective indifference to the use of solitary confinement, solitary confinement is fitting punishment for any number of crimes. Lock them in the hole and throw away the key! It is the just dessert for despicable, unforgivable acts like torture, rape, and murder—or so people think who not just tolerate the use of solitary but commend it.

And then there are people who give no thought whatsoever to this practice. For them it is not even on their radar, but, if asked, they would write it off as fitting punishment. They do not see its harms and do not care to learn anything about them. The situation is this: The recipients of solitary have such little moral status that isolation gets rolled in as an extension of the punishment.

So, what would Aristotle think? To answer this question, we need to look at his concept of justice and see how that affects the use of punishment. Aristotle links justice to what is lawful. He says, "The unjust is divided into the lawless and the unfair, and the just into the lawful and the fair" (*NE* 2019, p. 83). He also notes that justice is the exercise of the whole of virtue, and injustice of the whole of vice (2019, p. 83). And "For most lawful actions, we might say, are those produced by virtue as a whole, for the law prescribes living in accord with each virtue and forbids living in accord with each vice" (2019, p. 83).

7.16 Retributive Justice

In the discussion of justice in the *Nicomachean Ethics,* Aristotle pays particular attention to distributive and retributive (rectificatory) justice. When it comes to punishment retributive justice is a central concern. For some, the idea of *lex talionis*—" eye for an eye"—is a fitting penal response, especially with crimes of violence. It is considered a payback, a response in kind to the offense in question (see also Sect. 4.3).

Philosopher Alec Walen (2020) argues that "retributive justice must ultimately be justified in a larger moral context that shows that it is plausibly grounded in, or at least connected to, other deeply held moral principles." This fits with Aristotle's view of justice as linked to what is lawful and fair. The larger moral context, as Walen points out, matters. Justice should not be an outlier, on the edge of what it takes to lead a virtuous and meaningful life.

In Walen's view an inquiry into justice should take into account two background concepts. These are punishment and the types of wrongs for which punishment would be deserved. The former is a key issue when it comes to solitary confinement. Specifically, how do we determine *appropriate* punishment and where does solitary confinement fit?

However much the thought of suitable punishment is appealing, putting it into effect is not easily done. We would need to decide if solitary confinement could constitute *just* punishment. Obviously, solitary confinement is seen as an option, particularly for the most heinous crimes. All the Supermax prisons show an indifference if not acceptance of long-term isolation to punish the offenders. Serial killers and suspected terrorists, for instance, get little sympathy when considering the use of solitary. However, a key question is, "Is solitary confinement just punishment and, if so, when?"

Joshua Manson, speaking for Solitary Watch, brings up an important concern. Specifically, the UN Special Rapporteur on Torture, Juan E. Méndez, presented a report to the General Assembly in 2011 comparing solitary confinement practices around the world. The report, for the first time, declared that solitary confinement may amount to cruel, inhuman, or degrading treatment and in some cases torture, and may thus, under certain conditions, be prohibited under international law. Méndez called for a categorical ban on subjecting juveniles and people with mental illness to solitary confinement, and to end the practice of prolonged and indefinite solitary confinement (Manson 2016).

If the United Nations is justified in condemning solitary confinement as cruel, inhuman, and degrading treatment and a form of torture, its use as punishment should cease. Aristotle would agree.

7.17 Conclusion

Looking at justice, Aristotle would say that which is just must be both lawful and fair, and that which is unjust is both lawless and unfair. When we consider the harms of solitary confinement, we may wonder how it can be fair even if it is lawful. Aristotle puts the two conjuncts of 'lawful' and 'fair' together. However, that which is lawful may not in fact be fair, though Aristotle would argue that it should be.

Aristotle contends that "whatever is unfair is lawless, but not everything lawless is unfair" (*NE,* 2019, p. 83). We might add that whatever is lawful can be unfair if the laws need to be amended to achieve fairness. That is the case with solitary confinement.

The extreme and severe isolation of solitary confinement, other than for a brief period, does not seem just and cannot succeed. The individual suffering and collective harm to the community have crossed a moral threshold. The door to prolonged solitary confinement must close. Aristotle would second that recommendation.

References

Aristotle. 2019. *Nicomachean ethics*. 3rd ed. Trans. T. Irwin. Indianapolis: Hackett Publishing.

Associated Press. 2023, June 11. Unabomber' Ted Kaczynski died by suicide in prison. *The Guardian* (UK).

Casella, Jean, and James Ridgeway. 2017, November 27. Five unforgettable stories from inside solitary confinement. *Solitary Watch.* https://solitarywatch.org/2017/11/27/five-unforgettable-stories-from-inside-solitary-confinement-2/

Graham, Lorie M. 1995–1996. Aristotle's ethics and the virtuous lawyer: A study on legal ethics and clinical legal education. *Journal of the Legal Profession* 20. https://heinonline-org.msmc.idm.oclc.org/HOL/PDFsearchable?handle=hein.journals/jlegpro20&collection=journals&section=5&id=11&print=section&sectioncount=1&ext=.pdf&nocover=&display=0

Hall, Edith. 2018. *Aristotle's way*. New York: Penguin Books.

Hattery, Angela J., and Earl Smith. 2023. *Way down in the hole*. New Brunswick: Rutgers University Press.

Homiak, Marcia. 2019, April 15. Moral character. *Stanford Encyclopedia of Philosophy*. https://plato.stanford.edu/entries/moral-character/

Irwin, Terence. 2019. Introduction. In *Nicomachean ethics*, 3rd ed. Indianapolis: Hackett Publishing.

Kraut, Richard, 2022, Fall. Aristotle's ethics. *The Stanford Encyclopedia of Philosophy*. https://plato.stanford.edu/entries/aristotle-ethics/

Manson, Joshua. 2016, October 28. UN report compares solitary confinement practices in the U.S. and around the world. *Solitary Watch.*

Putnam, Hilary. 1983. Taking rules seriously—A response to martha nussbaum. New literary history, Vol. 15, No. 1. *Literature and/as Moral Philosophy*. John Hopkins University Press.

Scott, Hannah K.et al. 2023, July 10. Behavior modification. *PubMed*. https://pubmed.ncbi.nlm.nih.gov/29083709/

Shalev, Sharon. 2009. *Supermax: Controlling risk through solitary confinement*. Portland: Willan Publishing.

Walen, Alec. 2020. Retributive justice. *Stanford Encyclopedia of Philosophy*. https://plato.stanford.edu/entries/justice-retributive/.

Chapter 8
John Rawls: On Justice

Contents

8.1 Introduction

Following in the footsteps of Immanuel Kant, John Rawls took the path of Deontological Ethics into the territory of justice. The result was his groundbreaking *A Theory of Justice*. His goal was to counter Utilitarianism in its influence on individual and societal decision-making.

In his preface to the revised edition Rawls says, "I wanted to work out a conception of justice that provides a reasonably systematic alternative to Utilitarianism, which in one form or another has long dominated the Anglo-Saxon tradition of political thought." He adds, "The primary reason for wanting such an alternative is the weakness, so I think, of Utilitarianism doctrine as a basis for the institutions of constitutional democracy." (Rawls 1999, xi–xii). With that in mind, Rawls set a goal of achieving justice as fairness.

In his opinion Utilitarianism did not do the job, so, we needed another approach. "In particular," Rawls says, "I do not believe that Utilitarianism can provide a satisfactory account of the basic rights and liberties of citizens as free and equal persons,

W. Teays, *Solitary Confinement*, Library of Public Policy and Public Administration 20, https://doi.org/10.1007/978-3-031-96566-1_8

a requirement of absolutely first importance for an account of democratic institutions." (1999, xii)

His quest had two main objectives. The first was to produce a convincing account of basic rights and liberties and the second was to integrate that with a principle of fair equality of opportunity (1999, xii). Once these two principles were in place, Rawls contends, the aim of justice as fairness could be achieved.

One of the main advantages of Rawls' quest for justice is in addressing inequities like solitary confinement, which has subjected thousands of people to near-total isolation and sensory deprivation. In this chapter we will see what Rawls would think. We will start with his theoretical framework and then consider its application to solitary confinement.

8.2 Ethical Framework

Concerns about justice challenge us—as with a dispute over a neighbor blasting music at 2:00 in the morning or letting their dog bark for hours on end. As we know, minor issues can mushroom into major irritations or even violence. Think of protests and uprisings, or accusations of corruption on the part of politicians. The wrongdoers may or may not get their "just desserts."

And so, we ask, "What *are* just desserts?" We speak of the concept as a combination of *just* and *what is deserved* in terms of what someone has coming to them. For example, a thief may justly deserve punishment in proportion to the severity of the offense. And charitable people may deserve praise or rewards for their good deeds. How can we be sure that justice has been served? How can we decide if it was appropriately lenient or punitive? We need a system to sort things out—a structure to help guide us to ethically defensible actions.

John Rawls is an ethicist we can turn to for guidance. He considers the concept of justice and sets out principles of fairness, with his focus extending from individuals to institutions. His approach helps us examine the treatment of justice and revenge with respect to solitary confinement, as we will see in this chapter.

8.3 "Justice as Fairness"

Rawls would not think much of "just desserts." As a Deontologist, Rawls emphasizes moral duty and intentions over goals or ends. That does not mean he is blind to foreseeable consequences but allowing them to guide decision-making would be wrong-headed. He would cringe at the idea of revenge being mistaken for justice.

Rawls was influenced by Immanuel Kant in universalizing ethical decision-making and thinking what is just should be lawful and fair. The effects of Kant's categorical imperatives can be seen in Rawls' work. Preserving human rights acquires utmost importance. Rawls asserts that "in a just society the basic liberties are taken for granted and the rights secured by justice are not subject to political bargaining or to the calculus of social interests." (1971/1999, 25) Consequently, his Deontological theory is distinguished from Utilitarianism with respect justice as fairness.

Rawls contends that "Utilitarianism is a Teleological theory [one focused on end goals] whereas justice as fairness is not." He explains: "By definition… justice as fairness is a Deontological theory, one that either does not specify the good independently from the right or does not interpret the right as maximizing the good." (1971/1999, 26) Furthermore, Utilitarianism is not individualistic. That is another reason to deny Utilitarianism a place in his theory.

Individual rights and institutional policies are key concerns of Rawls. His *A Theory of Justice* draws from both Deontological and Virtue Ethics to address injustice. With a motto of "justice as fairness," Rawls tackles such questions as: What do we owe one another as fellow humans? What am I obliged to do for you, if you are needy, a victim of prejudice, or down on your luck? Should we protest when institutions like colleges, hospitals, schools, and prisons have racist or discriminatory policies? How should we structure them to minimize inequities? For Rawls, "A just social system defines the scope within which individuals must develop their aims, and it provides a framework of rights and opportunities of the means of satisfaction within and by the use of which these ends may be equitably pursued." (1971/1999, 28)

Rawls was determined to flesh out a just social system. He contended that "The priority of justice is accounted for, in part, by holding that the interests requiring the violation of justice have no value." (1971/1999, 28) Examine the way society and its institutions function says Rawls, and then we can address injustice.

This advice resonates with solitary confinement. Its role in society and institutions like prisons, detention facilities and schools cry out for attention. Rawls would insist on taking steps, so laws, regulations, policies, and procedures are as fair as possible. As a result, "An individual who finds that he enjoys seeing others in positions of a lesser liberty understands that he has no claim whatsoever to this enjoyment." (1971/1999, 27) There can be no enjoyment in regarding or treating others as lessor or with a lower moral status and, therefore, Rawls wants nothing to do with such a stance.

His recommendation is as follows: To reduce the likelihood of bias, try not to be influenced by social, religious, or political connections or affiliations. Justice demands that we shelf personal interests when crafting a vision of social justice. Rawls thought this would provide an effective method of constructing a just society. He called it a "veil of ignorance." (1971/1999, 11)

8.4 Adopting a Veil of Ignorance

Starting with both Kant's and Aristotle's assumption that we are dealing with rational moral agents, Rawls wants to free decision-making of partiality and prejudice. "Somehow," he argues, "we must nullify the effects of specific contingencies, which put men at odds and tempt them to exploit social and natural circumstances to their own advantage." (1971/1999, 118) Accomplishing this goal requires distancing ourselves from biases by employing the veil of ignorance. Rawls sees it like a type of blinders restricting our vision, thus shaping our decision-making and moral reasoning.

The veil of ignorance requires we:

- Set aside personal traits such nationality, gender, religion, and race to minimize attachments and affiliations that might interfere with fair decision-making.
- Clear the deck. We then stand a better chance at arriving at a just policy without being swayed by special interests.

"It is assumed, then, that the parties do not know certain kinds of particular facts," suggests Rawls. He adds, "First of all, no one knows his place in society, his class position or social status; nor does he know his fortune in the distribution of natural assets and abilities, his intelligences, strength, and the like." (1971/1999, 118)

Moreover, the veil of ignorance also screens out specific information about what society is like right now and, thus, minimizes that distraction. We can then get a clearer view of the permanent features of a just social system, notes philosopher Leif Wenar (2021).

With the veil of ignorance in place, "As far as possible, then, the only particular facts which the parties know," Rawls claims, "is that their society is subject to the circumstances of justice, and whatever this implies. It is taken for granted, however, that they know the general facts about human society." (1971/1999, 119) This allows a social context for which justice has a place. Within that context the veil of ignorance can be put to work.

Rawls wants to ensure a degree of objectivity and detachment on the part of decision-makers. He thinks the veil of ignorance will accomplish this goal; but critics worry that the cost may be too high. For example, Karen Sihra of the Ontario (Canada) Institute for Studies in Education contends that, "Rawls' 'veil of ignorance' proposes that we willingly leave our subjectivities behind in an effort to determine the 'best reasons,'" Sihra argues. She thinks that it will be dehumanizing and lead to a disengagement that some may find oppressive (Sihra 2004).

Rawls would disagree. He believes we can become more objective if we free ourselves from personal interests and affiliations. Avoid such distractions as self-interest or anything else that would impede fair-mindedness. In so doing, we can put Rawls' justice principles to work. That is where we will now turn.

Rawls Three Principles

The Principle of Equal Liberty

Each person should have an equal right to the most extensive system of liberties compatible with a similar system of liberty for all.

→ *Universalize human rights.*

The Principle of Equality of Fair Opportunity

People with similar abilities/skills should have equal access to offices and positions under conditions of equality of fair opportunity.

→*Provide equal opportunities.*

The Difference Principle

Social and economic institutions are to be arranged to maximally benefit those who are the worst off.

→ *Favor those who are most disadvantaged.*

These three principles form the core of Rawls' theory. The first principle, that of equal liberty, is meant to guarantee individual rights across the board. This principle echoes Kant's two Categorical Imperatives to act in such a way that it would become a universal law and always treat others as an end in themselves, never as a means only. Human rights should be attainable for *all* humans, so no one is relegated to a lower moral status. Furthermore, all humans should be treated with respect and dignity. No one should be left out of the equation, which is good to keep in mind about solitary confinement.

The first principle asserts that all citizens should have basic human rights and liberties. This includes freedom of association, freedom of speech, freedom of religion, the right to vote and hold public office, and so on. Wenar (2021) points out that this principle accords these rights and liberties to all citizens equally—justice requires equal rights for all, in all normal circumstances.

Rawls asserts that the basic rights and liberties and their priority should guarantee "equally for all citizens the social conditions essential for the adequate development and full and informed exercise of their two moral powers—their capacity for a sense of justice and their capacity for a conception of the good." (1999, xii)

The second principle is meant to guarantee fairness in access to institutions and opportunities. According to Rawls this requires "social and economic inequalities are to be arranged so that they are both (a) reasonably expected to be to everyone's advantage, and (b) attached to positions and offices open to all." (1971/1999, 53)

Rawls intended for the second principle to apply to the distribution of income and wealth and to the design of organizations that make use of differences in authority and responsibility. (1971/1999, 53) Those meeting the qualifications should be on the same level as any others having the relevant skills and experience.

The third principle is meant to resolve conflicts that arise over decisions as to who gets what. All relative factors being on the same plane, we should favor the least advantaged. By so doing, the society and its institutions will be more just and, thereby, strengthened—or so Rawls hypothesized. In setting out his third principle, Rawls points out:

> To see the full force of the difference principle it should be taken in the context of property-owning democracy (or of a liberal socialist regime) and not a welfare state: it is a principle of reciprocity, or mutuality, for society seen as a fair system of cooperation among free and equal citizens from one generation to the next. (1999, xv)

If the second and third principles are put in place, the results would be significant, as affirmative action shows. In addition, being placed in solitary for minor offenses would have to be justified, if not disallowed altogether.

Rawls sees his principles as reflecting Kant's second Categorical Imperative, namely, to treat others as an end in themselves, never only as a means. (see Chap. 6) He draws a clear distinction from the Utilitarian view that allows for people to be used in the service of societal interests, benefiting the majority. Rawls put it this way:

> To regard persons as ends in themselves in the basic design of society is to agree to forgo those gains which do not contribute to everyone's expectations. By contrast, to regard persons as a means is to be prepared to impose on those already less favored still lower prospects of life for the sake of the higher expectations of others. (1971/1999, 156)

"The Principle of Utility," Rawls claims, "presumably requires some who are less fortunate to accept even lower life prospects for the sake of others." (1971/1999, 156) Clearly Rawls finds this unacceptable. It is *not* okay. His Difference Principle addresses such inequalities in the very decisions that are arrived at.

Rawls' reflections here, along with his rejection of Utilitarianism, reveal the importance he places on equal liberty. Human rights are to stay in the forefront. In contrast, "in a public Utilitarian society [people], particularly the least advantaged, will find it more difficult to be confident of their own worth." (1971/1999, 156)

To achieve the desired state of affairs we may need to make adjustments, such as including an imbalance of current benefits that would lead to greater fairness in the long run. Philosopher Jan Edward Garrett (2002) points out that the Difference Principle means that the society may undertake projects that require giving some people more power, income, and status, than others (such as higher pay for those with more advanced skills), provided that the following conditions are met:

- *Best possible benefits for the most disadvantaged:*
- The project will make life better off for the people who are now worst off, for example, by raising the living standards of everyone in the community and empowering the least advantaged persons to the extent consistent with their well-being.
- *No discriminatory access:*
- Access to the privileged positions is not blocked by discrimination according to irrelevant criteria.

The Difference Principle expresses a positive ideal, an ideal of social unity, says Wenar. Rawls would agree. Moreover, in a society satisfying the Difference Principle, "citizens know that their economy works to everyone's benefit, and that those who were lucky enough to be born with greater natural potential are not getting richer at the expense of those who were less fortunate." (Wenar 2021) The end game is to balance the scales as much as possible.

Justice comes in different sizes and shapes. There are three major kinds: (1) Distributive justice, (2) Retributive justice, and (3) Compensatory justice. Distributive justice is about allocating rewards and burdens (think of Social Security and public education). Retributive justice is about punishment for breaking a rule or law (think of a speeding ticket or a fine for not wearing seatbelts). And Compensatory justice is about restitution for suffering a harm (think of food poisoning from listeria or salmonella).

As far as retribution goes, Rawls claims that,

> In a reasonably well-ordered society those who are punished for violating just laws have normally done something wrong. This is because the purpose of the criminal law is to uphold basic natural duties, those which forbid us to injure other persons in their life and limb, or to deprive them of their liberty and property, and punishments are to serve this end. (1971/1999, 276)

8.5 Revenge

To get a sense of Rawls' notion of justice, it helps to see what lies on the margins and what falls over the edge—such as vigilantism and revenge. Many acts of revenge are rooted in a frustration that spills over into rage, leaving justice far behind.

First, note that people often connect revenge with justice, under the mistaken assumption that they are linked. Think of movies like "The Brave One" and "John Wick" where the protagonist is out for revenge for harms they suffered. We frequently read about vigilantes—when someone decides the law is too disreputable or undependable to avenge a wrong and so they take matters into their own hands.

As we learned from Aristotle, such extremes lead to nothing good. Once ignited, rage can be explosive and, so, it is not surprising that revenge should result. It is easy to equate revenge with justice, as vigilantes do, but ethicists think it prudent to take a step back and ratchet down the rhetoric and the emotions. Impulsive reactions to perceived wrongs can rarely be thought morally permissible.

Revenge, as we saw earlier, is a mutated attempt at retributive justice. Retribution and revenge often rest on an "eye for an eye" rationale. The idea is that the perpetrator should suffer a similar loss—if not physically, at least psychologically. This is revenge taken to the extreme. Think about it. Do we want a society where citizens buy guns and hit the streets, ready to terminate those who evade the system? Rawls would be aghast at people adopting the role of judge and executioner.

Sympathies aside, Rawls would say that, in sidestepping the law, we abandon the justice system. This is fundamentally ill-advised. He would tell us to have more faith in the system and have a system that is just. Revenge and vigilantism are not the solution.

Rawls, like Kant before him, puts rationality in the foreground. He contends that we should disregard any attachments that prejudice our thinking. Otherwise, it will be hard to obtain justice. Rawls would contend that revenge, no matter how enticing, is not the path to justice. Justice extends beyond individuals wrestling with their conflicts to the community as a whole.

A key issue we face, then, is what we should do about solitary confinement. If we can extract the traces of revenge from the practice, can we consider its use an act of justice as fairness? Is there a way to balance the harms with the potential benefits? To answer that question, we should look more closely at the practice and listen to those who have experienced its effects.

8.6 Solitary Confinement

The toll—the human cost—of solitary confinement is heartbreaking. Those subjected to solitary confinement become more resentful, belligerent, and angry, points out psychologist Stanton Samenow (2023). They can also become depressed and self-destructive. Consider, for example, the remarks of one of the inmates at the Virginia Supermax prison the Red Onion:

> The monotony of the same thing over and over and over and over again messes with your mind …after I stayed in seg [segregation] for so long, being isolated it turned me worse. When I don't take my medicine, I cut on myself. That's what segregation did to me. (Jacobson 2015)

Others react similarly in turning their distress on themselves.

In terms of the number of those whose lives have been touched by solitary confinement, the present reality is alarming. Journalist Erik Ortiz reports on the situation in the United States: About 6% of the total U.S. prison and jail population on a given day in 2019 were placed in "restrictive housing"—solitary confinement (2023).

The reaction to these figures shows the level of concern. "Democratic Rep. Cori Bush, whose home state of Missouri counted nearly 12% of its total prison population in restrictive housing on a single day, said the report's findings underscore a 'catastrophe.'" Furthermore, "Inflicting solitary on one person is a moral blight on this nation,' Rep. Bush said. "Inflicting it on hundreds of thousands of people—disproportionately Black, brown and Indigenous people—is a disaster." (as cited by Ortiz 2023)

It is also a call to action: "We as public officials must act now to stop this widespread infliction of torture," Rep. Bush asserts (Ortiz 2023). Her plea emphasizes the gravity of the situation. It is a problem long overdue for attention and change.

Rawls would oppose the widespread use of solitary confinement. He would condone President Obama's move in 2016 to ban its use on juveniles in the federal prisons. Given it could lead to "devastating, lasting psychological consequences," said Obama, this policy change was warranted, as journalist Michael D. Shear notes (2016). It is especially advisable given solitary confinement "has been linked to depression, alienation, withdrawal, a reduced ability to interact with others and the potential for violent behavior," as Obama points out. In fact, "Some studies indicate that it can worsen existing mental illnesses and even trigger new ones," Obama says (Shear 2016).

Obama cites the case of 16-year-old Kalief Browder, accused of stealing a backpack and sent to Rikers Island in New York to await trial. He was held in solitary confinement for nearly two years. Browder was released in 2013 without having stood trial, but he committed suicide after struggling with the "trauma of being locked up alone for 23 hours a day," according to Obama (Shear 2016). Isolation crushed him.

Such self-destructive tragedies made banning the solitary confinement of juveniles all the more pressing, thus justifying Obama's policy decision. Since then, most states have followed suit in prohibiting or limiting the use of solitary confinement and/or shackles on juveniles, according to Anne Teigen (2022) of the National Conference of State Legislatures (NCSL). Rawls would be on board with this change. He would fully support Obama's decision to ban the use of solitary on juveniles in federal prisons and would favor its extension to the treatment of adults.

Of course, Kalief Browder is not the only one who self-destructed because of the extreme isolation of solitary. Example after example illustrate its harms. We get a sense of that—the sheer misery—when we listen to the voices of those who have been touched by the practice. Here are a few:

- "I feel like I've been buried alive in the ground."
- "You just have nobody, you're all alone."
- "That's the way I feel. Forgotten."
- "I hate it."
- "Being in that 8 by 10 cell 23 hours a day, that's a challenge."
- "Ask yourself, could I live in a bathroom for 10 years?"
- "If the inmate is not careful, they adapt to it and start becoming antisocial and become crazy. They go mad."

These are the words of "lifers" most of whom were at the Red Onion prison. In an interview for the documentary *Solitary: Inside the Red Onion Prison,* they conveyed their despair. (Jacobson 2015) The reality of this existence? As one "offender" (as some Corrections Officers call inmates) pointed out in the documentary, the window in his cell had frosted glass. He lamented the fact that he could not even see a tree—he could not see outside. The natural environment was closed to him.

It is an existence of utter hopelessness—a catalyst to mental illness and suicidal tendencies. Problems with the use of solitary confinement are serious and deeply entrenched. Such examples lead to the question: Is solitary confinement the kind of policy and Supermax prisons, where the inmates are in solitary, the kind of institutions that should be sustained? Do they bring justice and fairness?

8.7 Racism

A 2006 Yale University study of prison racism by law professor Judith Resnik made it clear that there were disparities around race in the use of solitary confinement in both federal and state prisons notes journalist Juleyka Lantigua-Williams (2016). She observes that some of the states where a large amount of the overall population are Latinos have significant racial disparities (2016). Consider the following examples:

> In California, Latinos made up 42 percent of the general prison population, but 86 percent of those in solitary confinement. Whites, by contrast, were 22 percent of the general population, but only nine percent of those in solitary. And in Texas, Latinos made up 50 percent of those in solitary, but only 34 percent of the overall prison population. (Lantigua-Williams 2016)

Consider also:

> There are significant differences in the rates of solitary confinement among Blacks, whites, and Latinos in New York, *The New York Times* recently reported in an in-depth investigation. Blacks and Latinos were sent to solitary confinement more often and for longer intervals. "At Clinton [prison] … black inmates were nearly four times as likely to be sent to isolation as whites, and they were held there for an average of 125 days, compared with 90 days for whites…" (Lantigua-Williams 2016)

The question then is, what is to be done? What steps should be taken to address such forms of racism? Race-based disparities in the use of solitary confinement have had a broad impact. "It's a problem for everybody, and the way to fix the problem, and fix the problem for sub-populations, is to end practices that deprive people of sensory stimuli no matter who they are," Judith Resnik said. (cited by Lantigua-Williams 2016) Rawls would concur with Resnik's recommendation, as his Difference Principle would offer support. Victims of race inequalities are certainly disadvantaged in this situation.

We need to look carefully at the policies and practices. Rawls would surely acknowledge that it creates and sustains systemic injustice and has no place in a society with fairness as a goal. Rawls would find fault with the practice and the institutions that embrace it. We will start with the veil of ignorance and then turn to his three principles to see what Rawls would think.

8.8 Applying the Veil of Ignorance

As we recall, the veil of ignorance requires disentangling ourselves from our various affiliations, attachments, and other factors of self-identification. Strip them from our thought processes so we can neutralize our brains. As much as humanly possible aim for absolute impartiality. No longer think of yourself, your interests, and personal investments in terms of your age, gender, race, ethnicity, religion, political inclinations, economic class, nationality, and the like. All of the aspects and prejudices that accompany your personal traits must be shelved. Out with them!

Once that's *a fait accompli*, we can address social and ethical problems and devise policies that will be fundamentally fair and just. With the veil of ignorance firmly in place, we now have the clarity of mind to tackle the issues at hand.

What we find when beginning this process is that we can no longer be indifferent to policies like solitary confinement that are easier to tolerate at a distance and do not directly affect us or those we care about. What if you or someone close to you were isolated 23 hours a day for months, years or decades, devoid of human contact? It would be an unacceptable level of brutality—one of cruel and unusual punishment.

Law professor Michael Shammas warns us: "A criminal who hurts others degrades himself; a society that hurts others degrades itself. Let's avoid degrading either. For we—and even criminals—are worthy of more. For we—and even criminals—are fellow humans." (2016)

Considering the extreme isolation stretching beyond a few weeks, the label "torture" is *apropos.* Organizations from Solitary Watch and the ACLU to the United Nations have voiced this concern (see Chap. 14) The conditions are dreadful—truly inhumane. For example,

> "The typical cell is a room slightly larger than a king-sized bed for a prisoner to "eat, sleep and defecate," [social psychologist Craig] Haney said. The prisoners lose orientation and a sense of self, ... They sustain high rates of anxiety, stress, depression, and related disorders. (as noted by science writer Joel N. Shurkin 2014)

Along with the psychological effects, solitary confinement can lead to physical consequences that are long-lasting, if not permanent. Neuroscientist Huda Akil asserts that the deprivation of social contact and stimulation, as is the case with solitary confinement, has a physical effect on the brain; one obvious in autopsies. She reports that parts of the brain shrink, such as the hippocampus, a region for memory and navigation (Shurkin 2014).

Given the prospect of such harmful effects, could we be free of bias in applying the veil of ignorance? If we were, we ought not subject anyone to the extreme isolation and lack of meaningful human contact that comes with solitary.

8.9 Conclusion

Let us now put Rawls' three justice principles to use. Rawls' first principle seeks to universalize human rights. To do that, Rawls indicates, the system must allow equal rights to liberty and do so systematically. His second and third principles aim at institutions and, although Rawls did not turn his attention to penal reform, it is an institution for which his recommendations are applicable.

His three principles help us grapple with the justice issues about solitary confinement. First, it is obvious that "the defining feature of solitary confinement, regardless of what it is officially termed, is the absolute deprivation of human interaction," as sociologists Hattery and Smith point out (2023, 30) This is the reality of near-total isolation. In fact, in some Supermax prisons the doors to the cells, showers, and yard, as well as the wicket, are all motorized so a corrections officer can control them from a remote location (Hattery and Smith 2023, 32). The result is surveillance from a distance. In this way the isolation is magnified.

Try to imagine what it is like at the ADX Supermax prison in Florence, Colorado. Many ADX prisoners live in near-continuous solitary confinement inside a soundproof, 7-by-12-foot cell. That is a controversial policy that prison reform advocates have decried, asserts writer Jerilyn Forsythe (2024). They have no human interaction other than with the officers who move them to the shower or shove meal trays through a slot in the cell doors. The effects of such extreme isolation are hard to fathom.

"The Supermax is life after death," says Robert Hood, who served as ADX warden from 2002 to 2005. "It's long term" he observed. And "In my opinion," he said, "it's far much worse than death," as Ray Sanchez and Alexandra Field reported for *CNN* (2023). Given the number of suicide attempts by individuals subjected to solitary, it is obvious that Hood is not alone in his assessment.

We can see why the ADX Supermax is considered the most secure and severe prison in the US: "Inmates have little contact outside of guards and prison staff. They must wear leg irons, handcuffs and stomach chains when taken outside their cells—and be escorted by guards." Furthermore, "inside the cage, only the sky is visible." (Sanchez and Field 2023)

Jeremy Bentham would second ex-ADX director Robert Hood's assessment that "The architecture of the building is the control." Hood adds, "You're designing it so the inmates can't see the sky. Intentionally. You're putting up wires so helicopters can't land." (Sanchez and Field 2023)

Court documents detail some of the effects:

> Many ADX prisoners "interminably wail, scream and bang on the walls of their cells,". . . "Some mutilate their bodies with razors, shards of glass, sharpened chicken bones, writing utensils, and whatever other objects they can obtain. A number swallow razor blades, nail clippers, parts of radios and televisions, broken glass, and other dangerous objects." . . . Some inmates have "delusional conversations with voices they hear in their heads"... Others spread feces, other human waste and body fluids throughout their cells or hurl it at correctional officers." (Sanchez and Field 2023)

It is a grotesque situation. This leads Robert Hood to ask, "When you see a person disrobing, throwing feces at a staff member going by—is that mental illness? Is that an issue where they're self-destructing?" (Sanchez and Field 2023) You would think we could do better.

Those sentenced to life in prison without the possibility of parole may have committed heinous crimes for which life in prison may be the just desserts. Assuming life in prison is defensible, it does not follow that solitary confinement is justifiable, particularly with long-term segregation. That is an additional form of punishment. What is the justification for that? Is that the sort of punishment that any set of circumstances would warrant? If so, what might those circumstances be? Are there really no alternatives?

Rawls believes that the way institutions and organizations are structured can have long-reaching consequences. Fairness is fundamentally necessary for achieving justice and, so, individuals should have an equal right to basic liberties. That means a just system would have to be structured to minimize bias. Fundamental changes are needed for that to be the case. Those changes are long overdue.

The effects of solitary confinement on individuals as well as the society make it clear that justice has not been served. Given his goal to universalize human rights, Rawls would say it is time for the door to close on solitary confinement.

References

Forsythe, Jerilyn, 2024, July 17. *The Most Infamous Criminals at ADX Florence, Colorado*. 5280, https://www.5280.com/the-14-most-notorious-inmates-at-the-adx-in-florence-colorado/

Garrett, Jan Edward. 2002, September 3. *John Rawls on Justice*. Western Kentucky University. http://people.wku.edu/jan.garrett/ethics/johnrawl.htm/

Hattery, Angela J., and Earl Smith. 2023. *Way Down in the Hole*. Camden New Brunswick: Rutgers University Press.

Jacobson, Kristi. 2015. *Solitary: Inside the Red Onion Prison* (DVD).

Lantigua-Williams, Julevka. 2016, December 5. The Link Between Race and Solitary Confinement. *The Atlantic*. https://www.theatlantic.com/politics/archive/2016/12/race-solitary-confinement/509456/

Ortiz, Erik. 2023, May 23. New Report Reveals Over 122K Are Held in Solitary Confinement in U.S. Prisons and Jails. *NBC News*. https://www.nbcnews.com/news/us-news/new-report-reveals-122k-are-held-solitary-confinement-us-prisons-jails-rcna84840

Rawls, John. 1971/1999. *A Theory of Justice*. Cambridge, MA: Harvard University Press.

Rawls, John, 1999. "Preface for the Revised Edition," *A Theory of Justice*, Revised Edition, Cambridge, MA: Harvard University Press.

Samenow, Stanton E. 2023, February 20. Should Solitary Confinement Be Extinct? *Psychology Today*. https://www.psychologytoday.com/us/blog/inside-the-criminal-mind/202302/should-solitary-confinement-be-extinct

Sanchez, Ray and Alexandra Field. 2023. December 6. What's Life Like in Supermax Prisons? *CNN*. https://www.cnn.com/2015/06/25/us/dzhokhar-tsarnaev-supermax-prison/index.html

Shammas, Michael. 2016, September 22. Against Solitary Confinement, *Huffington Post*. https://papers.ssrn.com/sol3/papers.cfm?abstract_id=3492530

Shear, Michael D. 2016, January 2. Obama Bans Solitary Confinement of Juveniles in Federal Prisons. *The New York Times*. https://www.nytimes.com/2016/01/26/us/politics/obama-bans-solitary-confinement-of-juveniles-in-federal-prisons.htm

Shurkin, Joel, 2014, February 21. Is Solitary Confinement A Form of Torture?! *Inside Science*. https://www.insidescience.org/news/solitary-confinement-form-torture

Sihra, Karen. 2004. Review of: Freire, Paulo: Education as the Practice of Freedom. In *Education for Critical Consciousness*. New York: Continuum. http://fcis.oise.utoronto.ca/~daniel_sch/freire/ks.html.

Teigen, Anne 2022, July 8. *States that Limit or Prohibit Juvenile Shackling and Solitary Confinement*. NCSL. National Conferences of State Legislatures. https://www.ncsl.org/civil-and-criminal-justice/states-that-limit-or-prohibit-juvenile-shackling-and-solitary-confinement

Wenar, Leif. 2021, Summer. John Rawls. *The Stanford Encyclopedia of Philosophy*, Edward N. Zalta (ed.) https://plato.stanford.edu/archives/sum2021/entries/rawls/

Part IV
Contemporary Perspectives

Chapter 9
Michel Foucault Punishment and Power

Contents

9.1 Introduction

We would be remiss to look at the evolution of punishment from the 1700's forward without examining the use of torture. As philosopher and historian, Michel Foucault emphasizes in his influential book, *Discipline and Punish: The Birth of the Prison*, the seventeenth and eighteenth centuries were sobering times for wrongdoers. Punishment often took the form of displays of torture and brutality for individuals thought guilty of an offense. These were years of public spectacles, notes Foucault, setting the stage for his study of prisons.

Not surprisingly, this takes us into the territory of Jeremy Bentham's Utilitarianism in the 1700's. It has had a leading role to play in Foucault's discussion. There we find Bentham's idea of a penitentiary centered on extreme isolation—solitary confinement. As we saw in Chap. 4, Bentham thought the construction of a prison that combined isolation and segregation with an omnipresent warden keeping tabs on the inmates would be an effective method of transformation. He called this a "Panopticon"—pan (all) opticon (seeing) —to convey a structure where people think they are being watched at all times. It rests on solitude, not physical torment. Inmates were not just isolated in Bentham's plan; they were also cut off from social interaction.

W. Teays, *Solitary Confinement*, Library of Public Policy and Public Administration 20, https://doi.org/10.1007/978-3-031-96566-1_9

Foucault observes that, with the passage of time, punishment has tended to become "the most hidden part of the penal process." (1995, 9) A consequence of this, he asserts, is that "it leaves the domain of more or less everyday perception and enters that of abstract consciousness… the publicity has shifted to the trial and to the sentence; the execution itself is [entrusted] to others under the seal of secrecy." (1995, 9) In that regard punishment no longer involves a public display of a bodily penalty, because the execution of pain takes place behind closed doors.

Consequently, the disappearance of public executions marked the decline of the spectacle. The public display of punishment was no longer desirable. (1995, 9–10) Physical pain was not to be the constituent element of the penalty. Bentham's goal was to "deprive the prisoner of all rights, but do not inflict pain." (1995, 10) This, then, is a double process: the disappearance of the spectacle and the elimination of pain. (1995, 11) How best to achieve that goal? You got it! Solitary confinement.

The Panopticon is perfect for privatizing punishment. The wrongdoer becomes the enemy of society. "He is nothing less than a traitor, a 'monster,'' Foucault points out. He asks, "How could society not have an absolute right over him?" (1995, 90) Foucault goes on to argue: "Every malefactor, by attacking the social rights, becomes, by his crimes, a rebel and a traitor to his country; by violating its laws he ceases to be a member of it." (1995, 90) All the more reason to isolate him and cut off human contact. Ostracize him. Furthermore, we must, Foucault asserts, "rid ourselves of the illusion that penality is above all (if not exclusively) a means of reducing crime. (1995, 24)

One of the points Foucault makes is that, in recent years, a number of prison revolts have taken place. Some were against the physical conditions of suffocating, overcrowded facilities, but there have also been revolts against modern prisons with isolation. Foucault says, "What was at issue was not whether the prison environment was too harsh or too aseptic, too primitive or too efficient, but its very materiality as an instrument and vector of power." (1995, 30)

Bentham's proposed solution is combining solitude with surveillance, so let's go there next. For Foucault, it is a journey into power.

9.2 Bentham's Panopticon

Foucault opens with a parallel between Bentham's Panopticon and the quarantine of a plague in the seventeenth century. The town was divided into quarters, with each one governed by an attendant who kept it under surveillance. One of his tasks was to make sure the residents stayed indoors. That entailed locking their doors from the outside. Attempts to leave were under the pain of death.

The result was a form of imprisonment intended to be in effect until the risk of the plague passed. With guards at the gates, "Inspection functions ceaselessly. The gaze is alert everywhere." (Foucault 1995, 195–196) Surveillance ruled. It was a grim situation, as Albert Camus' novel *The Plague* illustrates with a literary account.

Foucault describes the situation: "Everyone locked up in his cage, everyone at his window, answering to his name and showing himself when asked—it is the great review of the living and the dead… the slightest movements are supervised, in which all events are recorded." (1995, 196, 197)

Sound familiar? "Bentham's Panopticon is the architectural figure of this composition," says Foucault. "We know the principle on which it was based." (1995, 200). This is how it was to take place, turning the Panopticon into an image of surveillance:

> First, the architecture of the building itself: At the periphery, an annular building shaped like a ring. At the center is a tower for situating the supervisor.
>
> Secondly: "The building is divided into cells" for the placement of the individuals within the ring.
>
> Next, the arrangement: "All that is needed, then, is to place a supervisor in a central tower and to shut up in each cell a madman, a patient, a condemned man, a worker, or a schoolboy." (1995, 200)
>
> The separation of the cells: "They are like so many cages, so many small theatres in which each actor is alone, perfectly individualized and constantly visible."
>
> The end result: "Each individual, in his place, is securely confined to a cell from which he is seen from the front by the supervisor; but the side walls prevent him from coming into contact with his companions."
>
> And its effects: "He is seen, but he does not see; he is the object of information, never a subject in communication." (Foucault 1995, 200)

Subjects become objects. All social contact has been cut off—the isolation is firmly in place. Those held in solitary confinement were seen as objects to be locked away, no longer members of the society. Their moral status is negligible.

Marginalized and excluded from any meaningful communication, they are the living dead. The isolation is not just physical—all human contact falls by the wayside. The picture is of sequestered and observed solitude, as Foucault says. Their permanent visibility locks in the power differential between the warden and the inmates.

Consigning someone to a cell the size of a parking space, with no opportunity for relationships or any social dimension, their lives would be devastating. Bentham did not foresee the result of his invention becoming a reality. If he had he would have to rethink what had seemed such a bright idea at the outset.

So where does this take us? Bentham never saw his penitentiary plan put to use, so he had no idea what a disaster it would be. But if we catapult to the present, we find a widespread use of solitary confinement. If we look in penal facilities and high-security Supermax prisons, we see the Panopticon failing in significant respects. The idealism at the base of Bentham's vision dissipates when that vision takes shape.

9.3 The Tyranny of Power

Foucault explores the territory and its reliance on a tyranny of power. What matters, Foucault points out, is that the "wrongdoers" should know they are being watched. "Bentham lay down the principle that power should be visible and unverifiable," in the sense that they do not know exactly when they are being observed. However, they assume that it is an ongoing possibility; a 24/7 reality. The bottom line is that "one is totally seen, without ever seeing; in the central tower, one sees everything without ever being seen." (Foucault 1995, 202) Foucault puts *power* at the center of Bentham's vision. This is an emphasis he develops in assessing Bentham's vision of the Panopticon.

Foucault's observations of the Quakers' use of solitary confinement bears similarities to its recent use. In particular, "The prison, though an administrative apparatus, will at the same time be a machine for altering minds." (1995, 125) He was right about that. It does alter minds, though not as intended. It is certainly not to the benefit of the recipient.

You cannot read Foucault's discussion of Bentham's Panopticon without noticing his ongoing references to power and the degree to which he threads "power" into the picture he paints. The oppressive aspects of Bentham's ideal penitentiary—the Panopticon—do not escape Foucault's notice. As far as he's concerned, it is a demonstration of power in its most pronounced form—control. We can see that in the various examples:

- "The agent of punishment must exercise a total **power**, which no third party can disturb; the individual to be corrected must be entirely enveloped in the **power** that is being exercised over him. Secrecy is imperative, and so too is autonomy…" (1995, 129)

  → *This establishes the "omnipresent" warden as the one who is in control, with the inmates powerless in comparison.*

- "The major effect of the Panopticon: to induce in the inmate a state of conscious and permanent visibility that assures the automatic functioning of **power.**" (1995, 201)

  → *The construction of the penitentiary results in inmates feeling under constant surveillance.*

- "This architectural apparatus should be a machine for creating and sustaining a **power** relation independent of the person who exercises it, that the inmates should be caught up in a **power** situation of which they are themselves the bearers." (1995, 201)

  → *This establishes the force of the Panopticon itself—not just individuals—in preserving control over the prison population.*

- "The Panopticon is a marvelous machine, which, whatever use one may wish to put it to, produces homogeneous effects of **power.**" (1995, 202)

→ *The Panopticon penitentiary creates and sustains—enforces—power relations.*

- "It is an important mechanism, for it automatizes and disindividualizes **power.**" (1995, 202)

  → *The Panopticon strips the personal power from the inmates and isolates and alienates them from others.*

- "He who is subjected to a field of visibility, and who knows it, assumes responsibility for the constraints of **power.**" (1995, 202)

  → *The ongoing visibility leads to the controls being internalized, so inmates feel personally responsible for the effects of the Panopticon.*

- "The Panopticon functions as a kind of laboratory of **power.** (1995, 204)

  → *This recognizes the ways the Panopticon is a human experiment allowing the effects of power to be analyzed.*

- "The Panopticon "must be understood as a generalizable model of functioning; a way of defining **power** relations in terms of the everyday life of men." (1995, 205)

  → *The Panopticon itself governs the relationships in its scope by virtue of its construction.*

From all that Foucault sees, the Panopticon is an expression of power. He concludes: "The Panopticon presents a cruel, ingenious cage." It is "the diagram of a mechanism of power reduced to its ideal form." (1995, 205)

We should not underestimate Foucault's emphasis on power in assessing Bentham's Panopticon. 'Power' can be understood in two distinct and contrasting ways. One way to speak about power is in the positive as, for instance, in the word 'empower,' where it is understood as strengthening someone. Think of "The new policy empowers employees to be more innovative." In that sense the use of the term 'power' corresponds to 'power to do this or that.'

On the other hand, 'power' can take a negative form, as with 'power over.' In that regard 'power' is perceived as controlling or oppressive. It is that use that Foucault repeatedly refers to when discussing Bentham's Panopticon and its use is not just to prisons, but also to other institutions. He shines the spotlight on the oppressive aspects of power as an instrument of control.

Bentham thought the Panopticon had valuable uses extending beyond prisons to hospitals, asylums, schools, and factories. In his view all of these institutions would benefit from instilling isolation. Foucault points out that "In each of its applications, it makes it possible to perfect the exercise of power." (1995, 206) We see this in Foucault's remarks on the use of a Panopticon approach to a school in the 17th century. He states:

> *The architecture:* "The very building of the Ecole [school] was to be an apparatus for observation; the rooms were distributed along a corridor like a series of small cells...This infinitely scrupulous concern with surveillance is expressed in the architecture by innumerable petty mechanisms." (1995, 172–173)

> *The expression of power:* 'The disciplinary institutions secreted a *machinery of control* that functioned like a microscope of conduct." (1995, 173, my emphasis)
>
> *The result*: "The perfect disciplinary apparatus would make it possible for a single gaze to see everything constantly. …The power in the hierarchized surveillance…functions like a piece of machinery." (1995, 173, 177)

As far as Foucault was concerned, what Bentham dreamed up in the 1700's applied to the present day. The Panopticon model of power relations has had a much wider application and relevance than with penitentiaries, although Bentham sees penitentiaries as the prime example. Foucault puts it this way: "Our society is one not of spectacle, but of surveillance. We are "in the panoptic machine, invested by its effects of power." (1995, 217) In fact, Foucault ends his discussion of the Panopticon with this observation:

> The practice of placing individuals under 'observation' is a natural extension of a justice imbued with disciplinary methods and examination procedures. Is it surprising that the cellular prison, with its regular chronologies, forced labor, its authorities of surveillance and registration, its experts in normality, who continue and multiply the functions of the judge, should have become the modern instrument of penality? Is it surprising that prisons resemble factories, schools, barracks, hospitals, which all resemble prisons? (1995, 227–228)

9.4 Conclusion

Solitary confinement, as Bentham envisioned, consisted of isolation and segregation. Locked in a tiny space, deprived of social interaction for days, weeks, months or years on end can result in effects that are alarming and without any benefit, other than the incarceration itself. The society has removed the offenders, so they are out of sight and out of mind. This breeds secrecy, as Foucault contends.

We do not see the consequences of extreme solitude. We cannot easily weigh the harms with no Ethics Committee to oversee the policy. It transpires without the oversight fitting for a practice that would affect thousands of men, women, and children.

Foucault reminds us over and over again that the Panopticon, with its round-the-clock surveillance, is a picture of oppression. It is held in place by a power differential that is draconian in its scope. It is not a "power to" shaping either moral reformation or behavior modification. It is a "power-over" that strips its subjects of their autonomy and dignity. Foucault judged it to be a "cruel, ingenious cage." He considered it a symbol of the repressive, disciplinary society, the modern "society of surveillance." (1995, 208) No wonder he saw the Panopticon as a laboratory of power.

If we conclude nothing else from Foucault's inquiry, solitary confinement and the surveillance society Bentham held in such high regard should be relegated to the dustbin of history. As a method of punishment or discipline solitary confinement has little value.

Reference

Foucault, Michel. 1995. *Discipline & Punish: The Birth of the Prison*. 2nd ed. Translated from the French by Alan Sheridan. New York: Vintage Books.

Chapter 10
Beauchamp and Childress: Principles of Biomedical Ethics

Contents

10.1 Introduction

In 1979 Tom L. Beauchamp and James F. Childress set out what they considered the four basic principles of Biomedical Ethics. They are autonomy, nonmaleficence, beneficence, and justice—said to be the cornerstones of ethical decision-making. All four underscore human rights, particularly with respect to patient care. As we will see in this chapter, these four values also apply to solitary confinement and mental health concerns.

The first principle is autonomy. It is of fundamental significance in Western bioethics and the law. It is often held up as an ethical centerpiece, given the importance placed on individual decision-making.

W. Teays, *Solitary Confinement*, Library of Public Policy and Public Administration 20, https://doi.org/10.1007/978-3-031-96566-1_10

10.2 Principle #1: Autonomy

Beauchamp and Childress' first principle of Biomedical Ethics is autonomy, which they use to examine individuals' decision-making in health care and research. (2009, 99) Autonomy emphasizes self-rule (autos "self" and nomos "rule")— "free from both controlling interference by others and from certain limitations such as inadequate understanding that prevents meaningful choice." (Beauchamp and Childress 2009, 99)

In their view, most theories of autonomy see *liberty* (the independence from controlling influences) and *agency* (the capacity for intentional action) as the two essential conditions. (2009, 100) Obviously prisoners have limitations with regard to independence from controlling influences. To a great degree they lack the capacity for intentional action. Their autonomy is severely limited—particularly the case with those in solitary confinement. Their movement is constricted and opportunities for social engagement are negligible. In addition, they have few, if any, options for the use of their time. Inmates such as Albert Woodfox, remark on the boredom they suffer having nothing to do day by stultifying day. Some consider it a living death and become suicidally depressed and/or suffer hallucinations.

Just as it does for all of us, autonomy is crucial for our well-being. Being locked away from all human contact reduces chances of autonomy. Having more autonomous decision-making would improve the living conditions of those held in solitary.

The physical environment alone limits personal autonomy. Existing in a space the size of an eight-by-twelve-foot closet restricts physical movement to pacing back and forth and doing push-ups. Such an extreme living space and limited movement is hard to comprehend. It would certainly be unbearable.

Even worse are the social conditions. Correction: the *lack* of social conditions. Silence is the existential reality of solitary confinement. Those confined to solitary who yearn for a conversation often resort out of desperation to talking to themselves. That is why one inmate said he was "trapped in emptiness." So it is that policies and practices can work to compromise autonomous choice. Beauchamp and Childress observe that,

> The threat of exploitation is substantial in institutions where populations are admitted involuntarily, yet the fact that a person is coercively institutionalized or lives in a coercive institution does not automatically entail that each of that person's decisions is coerced. No reason exists why prisoners, for example, cannot validly consent to some research if researchers do not use coercive tactics in recruitment or make manipulative offers, such as unduly large payments for excessive risk taking. (2009, 135)

Bioethicist Jonathan D. Moreno discusses the use of prisoners in human subjects research in his book *Undue Risk: Secret State Experiments on Humans*. For example, prisoners were used in experiments on dioxin, malaria, hallucinatory drugs, and high-dose radiation, as well as other experiments undertaken by the U.S. government. Researchers decided in some cases that "only prisoner volunteers would satisfy the experimental requirements." (Moreno 2001, 30) Moreno points out that

"The inmates seem to have been thought suitable for some of the most dangerous and unpleasant tasks." (2001, 33)

Inmates were "thought suitable" because of their lower moral status. That the experiments were out of the public eye was likely another factor. Basically, the subjects were treated as expendable. "By the 1960s, at least half the states allowed prisoners to be used as medical guinea pigs," reports journalist Mike Stobbe for *NBC News*. (2011) Considering the value of personal autonomy, the essential conditions of liberty and agency should have been acknowledged. So, too, with issues involving informed consent.

A key ruling in the legal history of informed consent is *Schloendorff v. Society of New York Hospital* (1914) which established the right of self-determination. The New York Appeals Court ruled: "Every human being of adult years and sound mind has as a right to determine what shall be done with his own body." This decision put patient autonomy and self-determination on the map. It has continued to be a mainstay in court decisions involving informed consent.

Beauchamp and Childress point out the importance of autonomy in the work of both Mill and Kant, two of the most influential philosophers (see Chaps. 5 and 6) Specifically,

> Kant argued that respect for autonomy flows from the recognition that all persons have unconditional worth…To violate a person's autonomy is to treat that person merely as a means; that is, in accordance with others' goals without regard to that person's own goals… Mill's position requires both not interfering with and actively strengthening autonomous expression…. In their different ways, these two philosophers both support a principle of respect for autonomy. (2009, 103–104)

As Kant indicates, respect for autonomy is rooted in the knowledge that each individual has self-worth—as an end in themselves. It follows that prison staff, researchers, and medical personnel have a duty to honor the right of self-determination. That means prisoners have the right to refuse treatment and the right to withdraw from medical treatment or experimentation. These rights have been violated many times over. Jonathan Moreno cites numerous examples in his book *Undue Risk*. He points out the need to recognize ethical and legal boundaries with respect to personal autonomy and informed consent.

Furthermore, according to the IMAP/OSF Task Force, in 2004 policy at Guantanamo Bay allowed interrogators to use medical and psychological information about detainees to exploit their weaknesses in interrogation. Moreover, "It was reported the military interrogators were freely, assessing detaining medical records." (2013, xxii)

Individuals in solitary are at the mercy of others—from prison administrators to guards and medical personnel. Their autonomy and right of informed consent have not been given the recognition they deserve. All competent patients should have the right to refuse treatment. In detention facilities like Bagram, Abu Ghraib, and Guantanamo Bay this includes the right to refuse such degrading or humiliating practices as forced nudity, "rectal hydration," sleep deprivation, and force-feeding. Beatings were often common. "They used to tie us to this chair, our hands and feet, and then applied electric shocks. Sometimes they used it for beatings, too," detainee

Hajimumin Hamza says, recounting the torture he underwent during his captivity in Bagram prison between 2017 [and 2021], as Agnieszka Pikulicka Wilczewska reported for *Al Jazeera* (2021).

In her *New Yorker* article "The Experiment," Jane Mayer discusses the treatment of detainees at Guantanamo Bay. For example, detainee Murat Kurnaz contended that he had been "forcibly injected with unknown and debilitating drugs" (denied by U.S. authorities). His attorney, Baher Azmy, observed that, "The whole place appears to be one giant human experiment." (Mayer 2005)

The fundamental requirement of health professionals, Beauchamp and Childress assert, is to respect a person's autonomous choices, whatever they may be. Mayer notes that detainee lawyers had difficulty getting access to prisoners' medical records. (2005) Rob Kirsch, a representative for six detainees, contended that medical care is sometimes withheld or dispensed depending on a detainee's willingness to talk to interrogators (Mayer 2005).

"Respect for autonomy is not a mere *ideal* in health care; it is a professional *obligation.* Autonomous choice is a *right*—not a *duty*—of health professionals," state Beauchamp and Childress (2009, 107). Furthermore, "Prisoners, even terrorists, have a right to their medical records, according to federal laws, common laws, the American Medical Association, and court trials," as bioethicist Arthur Caplan points out (cited by Mayer 2005). With that in mind, let us turn to Beauchamp and Childress' second principle of Biomedical Ethics.

10.3 Principle #2: Nonmaleficence

The duty of nonmaleficence is in accordance with the Hippocratic Oath maxim "Do no harm." That sets a minimal standard of behavior: Whatever you do for your patients, at least do not harm them. The duty of beneficence (Principle #3) sets a higher standard by calling on medical personnel to maximize benefits for their patient and prioritize their well-being. Nonmaleficence and beneficence are companion principles, Beauchamp and Childress note. If possible, help others, do what you can to make an affirmative difference and address personal needs. If you cannot reach that standard, minimally do not harm them.

The message is clear. Medical personnel and prison staff pressured to enable abuse or mistreat inmates should adhere to the duties of beneficence and nonmaleficence. That means standing up to cruelty and mistreatment, intervening where possible, and reporting violations of human rights whenever they see them. By no means should prison wardens, guards, or healthcare professionals be complicit in abuse.

Beauchamp and Childress draw a distinction between harming and wronging. Wronging involves violating someone's rights as, for instance, if an insurance company improperly refuses to pay a patient's hospital bill, whereas harming a person may be a disease, a natural disaster, or bad luck (2009, 152). They point out some specific rules that draw on the Principle of Nonmaleficence. Examples they cite are (2009, 153):

1. Do not kill.
2. Do not cause pain or suffering.
3. Do not incapacitate.
4. Do not cause offense.
5. Do no deprive others of the goods of life.

Solitary Watch (2023) reports on the harmful conditions individuals face—and must endure—in solitary confinement:

- The material conditions of solitary confinement units force individuals into chronic ennui and idleness.
- The cells are usually smaller than a parking space, with small, high windows or are windowless.
- Some cells have fluorescent lighting that never turns off, while others are in total darkness.
- In addition to being deprived of visual and auditory stimuli, victims of solitary confinement are denied opportunities for intellectual stimulation.
- Extracellular programming (such as work or education) is usually forbidden, as are reading and writing materials, radios, and art supplies.

In their discussion of nonmaleficience, Beauchamp and Childress consider major life-death dilemmas that physicians face caring for their patients. These include withholding and withdrawing treatment, extraordinary (or heroic) vs. ordinary treatment, and killing vs. letting die. One issue they look at is physician-assisted death. What are the moral boundaries in active euthanasia; for example, in assisting a patient in dying? Assuming the request is voluntary, and the patient is competent, would it be justified to accede to their wishes? Would that be a "death with dignity"? How much pain and suffering should count when considering physician involvement? Need an imminent death be in the prognosis?

When looking at treatment vs. non-treatment, Beauchamp and Childress advise, "The principal consideration should always be whether a treatment is beneficial or burdensome, not what its classification is." (2009, 159) They argue that "The distinction between optional and obligatory treatment, as determined by the balance of benefits and burdens to the patient, is the pertinent distinction." (2009,159)

10.4 Applications to Solitary Confinement

This matter has greater application to those in solitary confinement than we might expect. For individuals in prolonged isolation, such as those like Ted Kaczynski with a life sentence in solitary confinement, the extreme segregation might drive them to attempt suicide, as statistics have borne out. Kaczynski did commit suicide. The fact is that the rate of suicide is significantly greater for those in solitary than not.

This raises an important question facing medical caregivers. Could a quality-of-life argument support physician-assisted suicide for those in solitary confinement? Consider the argument:

The Argument for Assisted Suicide for Those in Solitary Confinement

- Prolonged solitary confinement (more than 15 days) has been recognized by the U.N. as torture.
- To be condemned to a lifetime of torture is morally unacceptable.
- Anyone facing a lifetime of torture has a liberty right of autonomy and nonmaleficence to opt out.
- Quality-of-life considerations support the right to assisted suicide.
- In recognizing that right, assisted suicide should be permitted.

Before we go further let us recall what Senator John McCain had to say: "It's an awful thing solitary," he said, "It crushes your spirit and weakens your resistance more effectively than any other form of mistreatment." (as cited by Fetig 2011) It fails the quality-of-life test, particularly because of the lack of human contact.

McCain (2008) also said, "As far as this business of solitary confinement goes—the most important thing for survival is communication with someone, even if it's only a wave or a wink, a tap on the wall, or to have a guy put his thumb up. It makes all the difference." (2008)

To consider assisted suicide a legitimate right, we should factor in two issues. First, that this option differs from the death penalty, which is is a *terminal* punishment meant to fit the crime. It is *not* an act of autonomy—of preferring to die rather than enduring a life of torture. In addition, the death penalty is a decision made by others and not an autonomous choice on the part of the individual considering suicide.

Secondly, this is a quality-of-life decision. Those confronting a lifetime of the torture of solitary confinement should have the right to exercise their autonomy. And it is not just an issue of low social worth—it is also the lack of a meaningful existence. And, so, assisted suicide may be thought desirable for those in solitary, cut off from human contact. However, that conclusion calls for closer consideration. In Beauchamp and Childress' view, we can avoid opening the door to active, involuntary euthanasia by stating the criteria for a quality of life with enough precision to avoid that danger (2009, 170).

One way is not to confuse quality-of-life for the patient with the value of the patient's life for *others*, as Beauchamp and Childress emphasize (2009, 170). Though the general public may be indifferent to the subjects' quality-of-life concerns, the families of those in solitary are not. They have a role to play. "The President's Commission for the Study of Ethical Problems in Medicine and Biomedical and Behavioral Research recognize a broader conception of best interests that includes the welfare of the family." (Beauchamp and Childress 2009, 170–171)

The Commission points out that the *impact* of a decision may be considered in determining someone's best interests (Beauchamp and Childress 2009, 171). If the impact on the family weighs in, neither the loved one facing a life of torture in solitary nor undergoing an assisted death should factor into the equation. What then?

At this point we must ask: "Is there an alternative that bears consideration—a third possibility for those in solitary? The answer is "Yes." Per the recognition that prolonged solitary is a form of torture, surely there is a better course of action than choosing to die. Assisted suicide does not seem to qualify as "death with dignity" in this scenario. Is there any dignity in wanting to end your life because it is intolerable—physically, mentally, and psychologically?

10.5 The Argument for an Alternative to Assisted Suicide

The quality of life of those in solitary is unacceptably brutal due to the physical conditions of the limited space, the mental harms, and the lack of human contact. There are other ways to punish or confine someone without turning to the extreme of solitary confinement. After looking at Beauchamp and Childress' remaining two principles, we will return to this issue.

10.6 Principle #3 Beneficence

Beauchamp and Childress's third principle is beneficence. Whenever possible, they suggest, we should strive to do good. That duty is a call for moral excellence and for doctors and other medical personnel to do what they can to help their patients. Similarly, prison wardens and guards should show beneficence in their treatment and interaction with their inmates. At no point should they enable abuse or deceit—their own integrity is at stake.

Principles of Beneficence demand more than the Principle of Nonmaleficence "because agents must take positive steps to help others, not merely refrain from harmful acts," argue Beauchamp and Childress (2009, 197). They focus on two principles of beneficence: positive beneficence and utility. *Positive beneficence* requires providing benefits to others, whereas *utility* requires balancing benefits, risks, and costs for the best overall results (2009. 197). "In ordinary English, the term *beneficence* connotes acts of mercy, kindness, and charity… *Benevolence* refers to the *character trait* or *virtue* of being disposed to act for the benefit of others." (Beauchamp and Childress 2009, 197) That is an important quality to strive for.

Beauchamp and Childress observe that we are not morally required to perform *all* possible acts that would benefit others, as much beneficent conduct constitutes an *ideal*, rather than an obligation (2009, 199). Nevertheless, some of the moral rules of obligation are:

1. Protect and defend the rights of others.
2. Prevent harm from occurring to others.

3. Remove conditions that will cause harm to others.
4. Help persons with disabilities.
5. Rescue persons in danger.

Rules 2 and 3 are particularly applicable to solitary confinement, given the degree and duration to which it causes harm. Beauchamp and Childress' Principle of Beneficence calls for a need to address harm. As they suggest, rules of beneficence present positive requirements of action. "We are morally prohibited from causing harm to anyone." (2009, 199) This includes self-harm as well.

Inmates are not exempt from this prescription. That said, we are obligated to act nonmaleficently toward everyone, but we are not required to act beneficently toward *all* people. "Nonetheless," they point out, "we are obligated to follow impartially *some* rules of beneficence, such as those requiring efforts to rescue strangers when the rescue efforts pose little risk." (2009, 199) It would seem that acting beneficently toward those in solitary similarly poses little risk. Therefore, we should consider it morally advisable. We should also take steps to address self-harm as well.

According to Solitary Watch (2023), one study showed that people in solitary are seven times more likely to commit self-harm and six times more likely to commit fatal self-harm than those held in general prison populations. People held in solitary for any amount of time while serving a prison sentence are more likely to die of all causes in the first year after release, especially of suicide and homicide (Solitary Watch 2023). Clearly these are alarming statistics.

10.7 Beneficence and Assisted Suicide

Beauchamp and Childress cite a case that raises interesting issues. It centers on the first person—Barney Clark—to receive an artificial heart. Evidently Clark was given a key that allowed him to turn off the compressor if he wanted to die. He thereby had the means and the recognized autonomy to end his life if he felt "It isn't worth it anymore." (2009, 217)

Beauchamp and Childress ask if Clark's use of the key would have been an act of suicide. If he had refused the artificial heart in the first place few would have labeled his act a suicide. On the other hand, if he shot himself after getting the artificial heart, that act would be thought a suicide (2009, 217).

They concluded that, if Clark used the key and turned off the heart, the controversy would be whether it was an act of suicide, forgoing life-sustaining treatment, withdrawing from an experiment, or all of the above (2009, 217). They contend that, "If suicide is a protected moral right, then the state, health professionals, and others have no legitimate grounds for intervention in autonomous suicide attempts." (2009, 217) Autonomy rules.

Does it then follow that persons in solitary have a moral right to an *assisted* suicide?

If suicide is a legitimate choice, then there are few, if any, reasons not to permit an assisted suicide. However, it could be that no health care professional is willing to take part in an assisted suicide due to their own values and beliefs. What then?

Rather than seeing their assistance as a duty, there is a better choice; namely addressing the underlying despair that leads to suicidal thoughts in the first place. Surely there is a palliative care alternative to either continuing the solitary confinement or committing suicide. It bears concern for the well-being of the inmates/ patients and the medical personnel as well. Health sciences professor Amber Comer points out the position of the AMA:

> The American Medical Association (AMA) Code of Medical Ethics does not condone physician participation, calling the practice "fundamentally incompatible with the physician's role as healer." As an alternative to PAD [physician-aid-in-dying], the AMA advocates aggressive multidisciplinary interventions including emotional support and adequate pain control (2019).

At this fork in the road, we would benefit from putting Beauchamp and Childress' fourth principle in the spotlight. Let's go there next.

10.8 Principle #4: Justice

Beauchamp and Childress's fourth principle is justice. This is in line with Aristotle, who considers justice to be the overarching moral duty—one with vast significance. What follows from this? Well, justice entails fairness and consideration of all concerned. Philosopher Wayne P. Pomerleau offers this interpretation: "Aristotle says justice consists in what is lawful and fair, with fairness involving equitable distributions and the correction of what is inequitable." (2013) There are three aspects to this definition; namely what is fair, what is lawful, and what is equitable.

Beauchamp and Childress point out that "The terms *fairness, desert* (what is deserved), and *entitlement* have been used by various philosophers in attempts to explicate *justice.*" (2009, 241) As with Aristotle, they see justice as fair, equitable, and appropriate treatment due to people. In contrast, "An injustice involves a wrongful act or omission that denies people resources or protections to which they have a right." (Beauchamp and Childress 2009, 241)

Whenever possible, doctors, prison wardens, guards, and other staff should intervene to stop abuse and other injustices and do all they can to change the status quo. At times inmates have been deprived of solid food from days to months and many have been subjected to sexual abuse, sleep deprivation, stress positions, and more mistreatment.

Distributive justice includes "policies that allot diverse benefits and burdens such as property, resources, taxation, privileges, and opportunities." It refers to the distribution of all rights and responsibilities in society (Beauchamp and Childress 2009, 241). A "compelling example" that they cite involves human subjects in research—an issue we considered earlier in this chapter.

Up into the 1990's, note Beauchamp and Childress, concerns centered on risks and burdens of nontherapeutic research. With the advent of HIV/AIDS, therapeutic uses of research broadened the justice considerations. As a result, access to research became as important as protection from exploitation (2009, 241). "*Freedom to*" and "*freedom from*" were both seen as aspects of justice. With that expansion, the importance of autonomy, nonmaleficence, and beneficence were underscored.

Beauchamp and Childress point out the following principles that tied to distributive justice (2009, 243):

1. To each person an equal share
2. To each person according to need
3. To each person according to effort
4. To each person according to contribution
5. To each person according to merit
6. To each person according to free-market exchanges

Principles 2 and 5 are particularly applicable to those in solitary confinement. In light of the torturous conditions, those subjected to the practice need help. Beneficence is definitely in order. The subjects very humanity, as Kant would recognize, merits more attention with respect to harms than has been paid. That can change.

At this point Beauchamp and Childress turn to John Rawls. Rawls called for a framework of justice universalizing human rights and a system of liberty accessible for all. (see Chap. 8) As much as possible eliminate bias and prejudice in order to help those who are most disadvantaged. This understanding of justice has repercussions in terms of duties to uphold. That should include standing up against long-term segregation and isolation, which the U.N. recognizes as a form of torture. Rawls would recommend a stronger role for justice than has been the case in prisons for decades. It's time for an overhaul.

Rawls has the most celebrated egalitarian theory of justice, asserts Beauchamp and Childress. He argues that people should receive "an equal distribution of certain goods such as health care." (2009, 247). That is rooted in Rawls' first justice principle—to universalize human rights. Inequalities (as with income) are allowed only if they benefit everyone and are based on fair equality of opportunity (2009, 247).

Disparities like racism and sexism fall under the second principle—the fair-opportunity rule. And they are a problem. Beauchamp and Childress point out note that "Rawls considers social institutions—including prisons—to be just if and only if they conform to these two basic principles (2009, 247). They observe:

> Many studies in the United States indicate that Blacks and women have poorer access to various forms of health care in comparison to white males. For example, gender and racial inequities in employment have an impact on job-based health insurance; and the race and gender of physicians often play a role in the quality of patient-physician interaction (2009, 250).

There is no doubt that both racism and solitary confinement violate Rawls' two principles. Rawls would be aghast at what he would see in the conditions and treatment of those in solitary confinement.

10.9 Justice and Racism

The National Commission on Correctional Health Care cast a critical eye at the disparities and inequalities affecting those in prison and definitely those in solitary confinement. Take racism, for example:

> In the United States, Black people are disproportionately harmed by the criminal legal system, from from violent encounters with police to facing harsher bail setting and sentence length than white people. There is a distinct through-line in American history, beginning with slavery and continuing through vagrancy laws, convict leasing, sharecropping, and the "War on Crime" and "War on Drugs," that illuminates systemic factors leading to the disproportionate incarceration of Black people relative to white people.
>
> The U.S. population is comprised of about 13% Black people, well about 35% of jail residents are Black. … Black people have a lower life, expectancy relative to white people and fare worse than white people on a number of health indicators, including receipt of mental health care (The National Commission on Correctional Health Care 2024).

That's not all. Many prisons treat inmates like slave labor. Look, for instance, at the Draper Correctional Facility in Elmore, Alabama. Prisoners take part in a "work-release" labor program for private businesses. This work is not optional, as they risk disciplinary action if they refuse, reports Talmon Joseph Smith for *The New York Times* (2024). "Under Alabama prison rules, there are thin lines between work incentives, forced labor and "involuntary servitude." (Smith, 2024)

Inmate Carlos Anderson says, "You have no choice." "If you don't," he adds, "they're going to send you back to the camp and you get rolled up with a disciplinary charge… which prolongs incarceration or being made to work without pay at prison facilities." (Smith, 2024)

> Critics say the system perpetuates the racist legacy of "convict leasing," which lasted in Alabama from 1875 until 1928. It forced state prisoners to do uncompensated work for private companies, which then kicked back lease payment fees to the state. Prison labor, however, remains common, from California to Texas to New York,…
>
> Across the country, state and federal prisoners earn 13 to 52 cents per hour on average, ….Unpaid labor for inmates is still allowed in Alabama and a few other states. In Alabama, unpaid internal prison work can be assigned to those who have not qualified for or been assigned to work-release…. Some inmates work for state and local entities, at tasks like road maintenance, for about $2 a day—the rate Alabama set for prison laborers in 1927. (Smith, 2024)

That's not all. California voters rejected a measure in the 2024 election to ban forced prison labor. Journalist Sophie Austin notes that the constitution already prohibits so-called involuntary servitude, but an exception allows it to be used as a punishment for crime (2024). In contrast, Nevada voters passed the proposal.

10.10 Conclusion

The Commission on Human Rights of the United Nations asserts that "The right of everyone to the enjoyment of the highest attainable standard of physical and mental health is a human right…for millions of people throughout the world, the full realization of th[is] right…still remains a distant goal." (as noted by Beauchamp and Childress 2009, 264)

Philosophers Madison Powers and Ruth Faden put forth a basic premise about justice; namely, "Social justice is concerned with human well-being—health, personal security, reasoning, respect, attachment, and self-determination…. The justice of societies and of the global order can be judged by how well they implement these dimensions." (Beauchamp and Childress 2009, 265)

Beauchamp and Childress consider the job of justice—their fourth principle—to be closely associated with beneficence (2009, 265). We might note the degree to which justice is also tied to autonomy and nonmaleficence. The four basic values that Beauchamp and Childress highlight are not just basic—and vital—for Biomedical Ethics. They also offer guidance for the treatment—and harms—of solitary confinement.

We need to keep the duties of autonomy and nonmaleficence before us, hold tight to the duty of beneficence, and render help. That means standing up to unjust practices—intervening where possible, and reporting violations of human rights whenever we see them. By no means be complicit in abuse. There are lines that should not be crossed.

We should keep in mind what Jack Morris, a survivor of solitary confinement, has to say when we consider Beauchamp and Childress' four values and the importance of working for change.

> There are few forms of torture worse for the human soul than isolation. Solitary confinement is used to break people, and many who are exposed to it suffer permanent harms. It has been found to be damaging to the body, and the mind, and ultimately results in broader societal harms that have been documented (Morris 2024).

References

Austin, Sophie. 2024, November 11. *California Voters Reject a Measure That Would Have Banned Forced Prison Labor*. Associated Press. https://apnews.com/article/california-labor-prison-slavery-prop-6-election-e295b561651940e2b527d7f5128b1b53

Beauchamp, Tom L., and James F. Childress. 2009. *Principles of Biomedical Ethics*. New York: Oxford University Press.

Comer, Amber. 2019, June 1. Choosing Death Over Suffering. *Harvard Medical School*, https://bioethics.hms.harvard.edu/journal/choosing-death

IMAP/OSF Task Force. 2013, November. *Ethics Abandoned: Medical Professionalism and Detainee Abuse in the War on Terror, Institute on Medicine as a Profession*. https://hrp.law.harvard.edu/wp-content/uploads/2013/11/IMAP-EthicsTextFinal2.pdf

Mayer, Jane, 2005, July 3. The Experiment. *The New Yorker.* https://www.newyorker.com/magazine/2005/07/11/the-experiment-3

McCain, John S. 2008, January 28. Prisoner of War: A First-Person Account. *US News & World Report,* https://www.usnews.com/news/articles/2008/01/28/john-mccain-prisoner-of-war-a-first-person-account

Moreno, Jonathan D. 2001. *Undue Risk: Secret State Experiments on Humans*. New York: Routledge

Morris, Jack. 2024, September 25. Newsom keeps cruel solitary confinement policies in place. *San Diego Union Tribune.* https://www.sandiegouniontribune.com/2024/09/25/newsom-keeps-cruel-solitary-confinement-policies-in-place/

Pomerleau, Wayne P. 2013. Western Theories of Justice. *Internet Encyclopedia of Philosophy, Iep.utm.edu*

Smith, Talmon Joseph. 2024, October 26. Inmate Labor Tests the Limits on 'Involuntary Servitude'. *New York Times,* https://www.nytimes.com/2024/10/26/business/economy/prison-labor-alabama-hyundai.html?smid=nytcore-ios-share&referringSource=articleShare

Solitary Watch. 2023. Solitary Confinement and the Brain: The Neurological Effects: Fact Sheet #5. *Solitary Watch,* https://solitarywatch.org/wp-content/uploads/2023/06/SW-Fact-Sheet-5-Neurological-Effects-v230613.pdf

Stobbe, Mike. 2011, February 27. Ugly Past of U.S. Human Experiments Uncovered. *NBC* News, https://www.nbcnews.com/health/health-news/ugly-past-u-s-human-experiments-uncovered-flna1C9465329

The National Commission on Correctional Health Care. 2024, January 12. *Position Statements, Anti-Racism in Correctional Health Care*. https://www.ncchc.org/position-statements/

Wilczewska, Agnieszka Pikulicka. 2021, September 22. Life in Bagram the Eyes of Former Prisoners. *Al Jazeera.* https://www.aljazeera.com/news/2021/9/22/life-in-bagram-through-the-eyes-of-former-prisoners#ixzz8qMJwTA81

Chapter 11
Michael Boylan: The Impact of Worldviews

Contents

11.1 Introduction

Michael Boylan has had considerable impact on ethics by focusing on both the individual and societal level. His approach emphasizes personal and community worldviews and gives us useful tools for examining moral problems. Boylan follows Aristotle in grounding his ethical theory in values and in developing moral character.

Basing his work on two worldview imperatives, he lays the foundation for a just society. In this chapter we will look at his ethical scaffolding and its application to solitary confinement. We will begin with the theory.

W. Teays, *Solitary Confinement*, Library of Public Policy and Public Administration 20, https://doi.org/10.1007/978-3-031-96566-1_11

11.2 Laying Out the Basics

Boylan sees the focus of ethics as its concern with right and wrong in judging or blaming a person's actions, while recognizing that ethics is more than that. It is a science he says—an activity studied rationally and systematically in seeking exact conclusions. (Boylan 2009, 3) This leads to the ownership and responsibility for the foreseeable consequences of our actions. The resulting consequences are judged "good" or "bad." (2009, 4) Moral responsibility rests on the free choice to do otherwise. If we lacked volition—free will—we could not be held accountable for what we say or do.

Boylan believes that each of us has a duty of self-reflection to examine ourselves. Such a duty of personal assessment affects the quality of our lives. He puts it this way:

> It is not enough to exist like a piece of driftwood floating on the sea of life. This is because free, rational deliberation is an essential part of our ability to be autonomous individuals. And unless we are autonomous agents, there is no real participation in ethics. (2009, 5)

Without the ability to perform free, rational deliberation, Boylan asserts, we give up a fundamental aspect of being human. Of course, Boylan is not the only one relegating autonomy to center stage. Many people, such as bioethicists Tom L. Beauchamp and James F. Childress, consider personal autonomy one of the most important values we subscribe to (see Chap. 10). This is especially the case in the West, where being autonomous is thought necessary for rationality to reach expression in our moral reasoning.

11.3 Heads I Win, Tails You Lose

In Boylan's seminal work, *A Just Society*, he examines justice with respect to both individuals and communities. He is guided by two theoretical frameworks that he considers imperatives.

One targets individuals; that is his Personal Worldview Imperative. The other targets groups and communities; that is his Shared Community Worldview Imperative. Together they provide the foundation of his ethical theory.

Our task in this chapter is to employ the two imperatives to put solitary confinement in the spotlight.

11.4 Boylan's Two Imperatives

Boylan starts out on the individual level with his Personal Worldview Imperative. It goes like this:

The Personal Worldview Imperative

> All people must develop a single, comprehensive,
> and internally coherent worldview that is good
> and that we strive to act out in our daily lives. (2009, 21)

This imperative has four components—completeness, coherence, goodness, and the necessary aspects for personal action. (2009, 22) Boylan explains these key elements as follows (2009, 22–25):

- *Completeness* aka *comprehensiveness* is a formal component."A personal worldview that is complete could confront novel situations in life and present an action recommendation." The best way to ensure completeness, Boylan says, is in developing goodwill. Both a rationally based goodwill and an emotionally based goodwill are necessary for our personal worldview to be complete. In his view "a large part if who we all are as *homo sapiens* is rational." (2009, 22)
- *Coherence h*as to do with rationality. We must not fall prey to either deductive or inductive contradictory thinking or acting. Boylan explains: "Deductive incoherence asks you to be consistent with what you espouse and do between various contexts in which you are presented with action choices." In contrast, he argues, "Inductive incoherence refers to a situation in which a betting house will always lose." (2009, 23). A person should not be deductively or inductively incoherent if they want to become the best person they can be. (2009, 24)
- *Goodness* has to do with the goodwill required to ensure completeness. Both a rationally based goodwill and an emotionally based goodwill are required to achieve completeness. Those are the senses of "goodwill" that Boylan focuses on. This connects us to a theory of good and to a coherent set of values. He asserts that "the best way to ensure completeness in a personal worldview is by developing goodwill." (2009, 22)
- *Action* has to do with putting these components into effect. We are enjoined to "walk the talk." We should adopt models that challenge us to be good and to achieve social justice. Furthermore, Boylan contends that every moral agent acting or potentially acting "falls under the normative force of the personal worldview imperative." (2009, 21–22). This then underscores its importance.

So how does this help us evaluate solitary confinement? Let us give this our attention. Boylan's goal with his first imperative is achieving clarity of reasoning. Crucial to that quest is making sure our values rest on a coherent foundation. Do they make sense? Do any of our values conflict with one another? And, if so, by what procedure are we to sort them and retain those that work together to express our beliefs? Can we reject those that undermine our set of values? Furthermore, how comprehensive and complete is our ethical scaffolding? What are its strengths? Any gaps or omissions? What do we need to do to patch the holes? If our reasoning is not solid, can we really support the practice of solitary confinement? What is the evidence?

This housekeeping is not a trivial matter. A great deal depends on the strength of our reasoning. Let us not forget that our goal is to have goodness as the basis of our theoretical structure. Can we say that is the case when it comes to solitary confinement? Is there goodness in the way it functions as a policy? And is our reasoning coherent and comprehensive? These are fundamental questions (and doubts) that we need to consider.

The issue is of paramount significance for our personal worldview, and our community worldview as well. With that in mind let us go to the latter.

11.5 Boylan's Second Imperative

Because there is more diversity in our society, Boylan observes that the Shared Community Worldview Imperative is not as exact as the Personal Worldview Imperative. Groups have more to factor in than do single individuals says Boylan. Just think how many perspectives we might need to consider. Here is the formulation of his second imperative:

The Shared Community Worldview Imperative

> Each agent must contribute to a common body of knowledge
> that supports the creation of a shared community worldview
> (that is itself complete, coherent, and good) through which social
> institutions and their resulting policies might flourish within the
> constraints of the essential core commonly held values
> (ethics, aesthetics, and religion). (2009, 25)

Key elements of the Shared Community Worldview Imperative are:

- A common body of knowledge
- A dialectical process of discussion among members and groups
- Social institutions responsible for setting policy
- Actions of institutions that reflect the members' core values
- Tolerance with the social diversity of the community (2009, 26–27)

Looking at the two worldview imperatives, Boylan points out this difference: "Many people are more inclined to take seriously the personal worldview imperative because it makes them more effective at achieving the prudential and ethical ends that they hold." (2009, 26)

That said, our community standpoint should not be discounted observes Boylan. Keep in mind that we live in a community and that affects our values and decision-making. Community membership has its ups and downs. It both enables and hinders personal liberty. "One cannot have one without the other," Boylan points out. Both worldview imperatives have a role to play in our lives. In addition, as we learned from Mill's Utilitarianism (see Chap. 5) our moral reasoning has roots in our community. So how does this help us evaluate solitary confinement?

To what degree is there a common body of knowledge about the practice? Do members of our community have a sense of the harms suffered by those subjected to extreme isolation and lack of human contact? Should we have faith in the reasoning? It would also help to consider how we are evaluating decisions by the various institutions responsible for setting policy and if there are periodic reviews of the practice and a consideration of the values behind that reasoning. These are important issues to take into account in analyzing the purpose and effectiveness of solitary confinement.

Both of Boylan's imperatives merit more attention than they have received. In examining the practice, we could see how the key values provide us with guidance and what else might warrant consideration.

11.6 The Four Virtues

According to Boylan, we need four virtues to kick-start the two worldview imperatives. These are wisdom, courage, justice, and self-control (2004, 44). They function as moral pillars of the imperatives. Here's how:

- *Without wisdom* we are morally blind and cannot hope to apply the lessons from the past to the present or the future.
- *Without courage* we are either weak or reckless. Neither state is helpful. We need courage to subject our reasoning, decision-making, and actions to scrutiny and make recommended changes.
- *Without justice* desire gains power and we lose sight of fairness and moderation.
- *Without self-control* we are either at the mercy of others or unable to pull back and take stock when things veer off course (Teays 2009, 98–99).

All four pillars are central to our value system. There is something to navigational terminology—like "staying on course" and having a "moral compass." It is no accident that people use these phrases when assessing individual and societal acts and policies.

Boylan's philosophical novel *The Extinction of Desire* offers this piece of advice in reflecting on one's "inner journey." "If I knew the direction, then the rest would no longer matter. If I knew the direction, then my way would be clear to me." (Boylan 2007, 174)

It takes wisdom and a sense of justice to know one's own direction and to have everything else fall into place. It takes courage and self control to find our way, guided by a sense of where we are headed—and why. It is a catalyst to introspection, seeing how neither deprivation nor indulgence work (Teays 2009, 99).

11.7 Distributive Justice and Retributive Justice

In *A Just Society* Boylan looks at distributive and retributive justice. He points out that distributive justice "concerns itself with the allocation of goods and services in a society (a sort of moral economics)." Think of public education and Medicare.

Retributive justice has to do with compensation for harm done. Think of a speeding ticket or a fine for abandoning an animal on the freeway. Boylan refers to it as payback—evening the score. It “concerns itself with the way we treat those who violate [our] rules.” (2004, 138) As Boylan notes, the word retribution means “to give back.” (2004, 181)

11.8 More Thoughts on Retribution

Boylan turns his attention to the retributive justice with regards to prisons and criminals. He argues that morality is fundamentally aspirational, contending,

> The Personal Worldview Imperative and the Shared Community Worldview Imperative are ideals to which we should aspire. These imperatives are about what we should do. It is part of our human nature to strive to be good. ...part of aiming being good means we aim at being as good as possible: seeking the best. The moment we give up on these ideals is the knell of death for humankind. (2004, 187)

However true it may be that “most souls will never turn themselves around,” says Boylan, we can provide opportunities for personal change (2004, 187). He emphasizes that “Even for those who because of their crimes will never be permitted back in the society, we should create prison environments that are structured in such a way as to make the possibility of such transformations more (as opposed to less) probable.” (2004, 187)

This view on Boylan’s part supports the argument that prison can be punishment in the deprivation of liberty. But putting solitary confinement on top of that in removing human contact is morally unacceptable. Our very humanity is rooted in society. To take that away inflicts grave damage to the individual.

As a result, Boylan is on the right track to affirm that “our model of justice must focus upon giving back to the criminal his own humanity.” (2004, 184–185) Boylan points out that, “Obviously, such a scenario rarely occurs in prison. Today’s prisons in the United States are schools of raising violence and bestiality to a higher level. They are not places of rehabilitation and rehumanization. But need this be the case?” (2004, 185)

When we add a component of solitary confinement, we now deprive a person not of liberty (they’re already in prison), but instead of the opportunity to be in contact with other human beings. However, the deprivation of society in this sense is incommensurable because it exists on a different scale than the deprivation of liberty. It therefore should not function as part of retributive justice.

Depriving someone of their liberty is one thing. Depriving them of contact with other human beings potentially for the rest of their lives bears no justification as a tool of retribution. Boylan contends that “In most cases the compensation element can be determined by standards to which most would agree.” (2004, 181) There is no obvious standard that would allow the deprivation of all social contact as commensurate with addressing an offense. The compensation of solitary is not proportionate to the harm done. There simply is no comparison.

These remarks on shunning by counseling psychologist Savin Bapir-Tardy (2016) are useful to bring into our discussion solitary confinement if we think of solitary as an institutional form of shunning. She does not link shunning to solitary—but we can. "The psychological consequences of being shunned can best be explained as a *social death penalty*" She explains: "The person then starts to attack their sense of self, which is also why shunning is often perceived as the death of personhood." (2016, my emphasis) As a result, "This leads to feelings of helplessness, hopelessness and worthlessness, depression, low self-esteem, suicidal ideations and self-harming behaviors," she asserts (Bapir-Tardy, 2016). Just as shunning can lead to despair and suicidal depression, so too can solitary confinement. The effects of being cut off from social contact are that severe.

11.9 Weighing Punishment

Boylan follows Plato in distinguishing two types of crimes (2004, 183)—crimes against a single individual (robbery, carjacking, murder, etc.) and crimes against the public, where the offender has injured the community at large (putting cyanide in Tylenol pills, flying planes into the World Trade Center, Virginia Tech massacre, etc.).

In the case of the harmed community, payback becomes more complicated. As Boylan says, "This is because it is unclear whether there is a positive good equivalent to what is lost that can be given to the whole society." (2004, 183) Clearly that's a major concern. What punishment would be proportionate? Boylan observes that

> In most cases, this would be impossible. Therefore, the state wishes to be rid of the offender. In times past, this took the form of exile and/or shunning. However, in our modern world, exile and shunning do not seem practical. Therefore, we have constructed houses of imprisonment in order to incarcerate these individuals. (2004, 183)

True, we have prisons to incarcerate the individuals. But how does solitary confinement factor in? Is it the modern equivalent of exile and shunning? How could we justify shunning via solitary confinement for thousands upon thousands of prisoners? Shunning went by the wayside for a reason. So, too, ought solitary confinement.

In Boylan's view, "Punishment of the right sort can help cure the soul and enable it to begin again." His advice? "This should be the goal of our criminal justice system." (2004, 185)

Boylan leaves us with this thought: "If criminals were to recognize the basic goods of agency through the exercise of the Personal Worldview Imperative, then they might be in a position to turn their lives around." (2004, 185) Boylan thinks that requires the prisoner to experience sincere regrets—which would "bring humanity to him." In fact, "This will both enrich the criminal and make him conscious of the misdeeds he has performed,"/says Boylan." "Consequently, this consciousness will be a continual punishment and healing agent to the criminal." (2004, 185) And if we recognize the values of the Shared Community Worldview Imperative, we might be able to transform the prison environment and its policies and practices.

11.10 Conclusion

There is a lot to learn from Michael Boylan's work on ethics and on his two imperatives. He would tell us to be guided by the four moral pillars of wisdom, justice, courage, and self-control when looking at the policies and practices of solitary confinement.

- Each pillar offers valuable benefits for applying Boylan's ethical scaffolding. A number of questions merit our consideration. Specifically:
- Did we demonstrate sufficient wisdom in determining the direction to proceed in our analysis?
- Will it lead to justice in the treatment of individuals subjected to solitary confinement?
- Did we demonstrate courage in putting an end to the injurious aspects of solitary?
- Did we take steps to make long overdue changes?
- And did we show self-control in our treatment of those most disadvantaged by the policies and practices we enact?

The journey is not a smooth transition from ignorance to awareness. It is easy to find ourselves going through one revolving door after another. Action of any kind requires a willingness to put our values and actions under a microscope. Boylan would recommend that we take the lessons to heart, so the set of values we adhere to is coherent, comprehensive, and good.

It is true that we do not always "get it" the first time around. The odyssey is not paved in gold. It has switchbacks, potholes, and perils. We need to reexamine our assumptions and shine a light on the harms we have been party to. It is time to confront our support or indifference to solitary confinement and see how Boylan's two imperatives can come to our aid.

References

Bapir-Tardy, Savin. 2016, November 11. The Practice of shunning and it's Consequences. *Sedaa: Our Voices*. http://www.sedaa.org/2016/11/the-practice-of-shunning-and-its-consequences

Boylan, Michael. 2004. *A Just Society*. Lanham MD: Rowman & Littlefield.

Boylan, Michael. 2007. *The Extinction of Desire: A Tale of Enlightenment*. Wiley-Blackwell: Malden MA.

Boylan, Michael. 2009. *Basic Ethics*. 2nd ed. Upper Saddle River, NJ: Prentice Hall Publisher.

Teays, Wanda. 2009. Extinguishing Desire: Not a Simple Plan at All. In *Morality and Justice: Reading Boylan's A Just Society*, ed. John-Stewart Gordon. Lanham MD: Lexington Books.

Chapter 12
Nel Noddings: The Components of Evil

Contents

12.1 Introduction

In her innovative book, *Women and Evil,* ethicist Nel Noddings analyzes evil from the perspective of Feminist philosophy. Her insights into the concept provide a useful framework for looking at solitary confinement. We will see how in this chapter. She sees evil as a trinity and characterizes it as having three components—pain, separation, and helplessness.

Each one of these concepts applies to solitary confinement and, so, they offer guidance for looking at the practice. There is pain (physical, psychological, and mental). There is separation in sequestering people and isolating them for lengthy periods of time, with little or no human contact. And there is helplessness in the effect of solitary in terms of autonomy (see Chap. 10) and human dignity (see Chap. 6). Noddings says, "To have control of one's body and mind is to be alive." (1989, 92) Unfortunately, such self-control is sadly lacking among victims of solitary. We see this with the first component—pain.

The original version of the chapter has been revised. A correction to this chapter can be found at https://doi.org/10.1007/978-3-031-96566-1_16

W. Teays, *Solitary Confinement*, Library of Public Policy and Public Administration 20, https://doi.org/10.1007/978-3-031-96566-1_12

12.2 The Evil of Pain

Looking at the three components of evil, Noddings observes:

- "The most basic form of evil seems to be pain." Physical pain, when it does not promise a better end state (right here on earth), is an evil we should avoid or relieve.
- Separation is evil because of the deep psychic pain it causes, and the fear of separation makes human beings vulnerable to all sorts of further evils.
- Helplessness too is associated with psychic pain, and we must consider its deliberate infliction a great moral evil. (1989, 118)
- "The fundamental evils seem to be a combination of physical and emotional pain—what we might call psychic pain, a pain that threatens our sense of being." (1989, 95)

She further asserts (1989, 95): *Physical pain* accompanied by hope or happy anticipation (as in childbirth) is not evil; only if physical pain overwhelms the more joyful aspect would we evaluate the occurrence as evil. *Physical separation* that induces emotional pain uncompensated by a sense of fulfillment, relief, or another positive effect is clearly evil to the one who experiences it. *Similarly, helplessness* unrelieved by carefree sense of happy dependence is evil. Thus pain, helplessness, and separation are the basic conditions of evil. (1989, 95)

What concerns her is the intentional infliction of pain; for instance, pain that accompanies abuse and cruelty. Noddings notes that it has been customary to separate natural evil from moral evil. She argues that "Suffering that occurs without the deliberate or negligent agency of human beings is construed as natural evil; violent storms, drought, disease, earthquakes, and natural death, are all examples of natural evil and part of the world we inhabit." (1989, 5–6)

That said, Noddings observes that we run into difficulties when we attempt to justify evil. "If, for example, we can find a justification for God's allowing us to suffer (or even for his inflicting pain on us), moral evil cannot be entirely identified with our infliction of pain on one another, for we too might be justified." (1989, 5–6)

Noddings contends that pain may be the first candidate for evil; however, pain, as noted above, is not always evil. She explains: "Useless and intractable pain we have called natural evil, but it might be even better simply to call it useless and intractable pain." (1989, 99). In contrast, "Real evil— moral evil—occurs when some agent causes such pain or fails to alleviate it when he or she is clearly in a position to do so." (1989, 99)

Noddings clearly differentiates pain resulting from natural causes from pain resulting from human actions or inactions. She says moral agency has a role to play in our response to the infliction of pain. She says, "The feeling should arise in us that we *must* relieve pain when it is in our power to do so, and certain we must not inflict pain unless we have an excellent reason"—which is not easy to produce. (1989, 99)

According to Noddings, there are two tasks in this regard. First, we should arrive at some sense as to relieving pain and, second, we should determine the conditions for which we are justified in inflicting pain. (1989, 99–100) In the case of solitary confinement—and torture—all three evil components of inducing pain, helplessness, and separation may come into play. There are physical, mental, and psychological harms, particularly in the use of prolonged solitary. And those harms can have a lasting impact.

Michel Foucault would say all three of these components of evil are the result of an expression of power (see Chap. 9). Those in control can—and often *do*—wield power over their victims, as we see in abusive aspects of solitary. One of the expressions of power is in the control of the other person. Such demonstrations of power are a reality of solitary confinement. The power differential is firmly in place.

Human rights activists and agencies like Solitary Watch, Human Rights Watch, ACLU, and Amnesty International track abuses and make public their findings and advocacy. They work in conjunction with the United Nations and the World Medical Association to address policies and practices resulting in or exacerbating helplessness and separation from extreme isolation.

On one end of the pain spectrum is the physical aspect of pain, which can spin out of control and escalate. "Whenever we actually inflict pain, we separate ourselves from the victims. If possible, we avoid their eyes," notes Noddings. (1989, 227–228) That is one way of distancing ourselves from the other person. As we saw in Chap. 3, hooding is an effective way of avoiding the suffering of the victims. Avoiding their eyes makes it easier not to feel empathy—their humanity is shielded by the hoods or sandbags. Their moral status then shrinks.

In Noddings' assessment "The pain accomplishes nothing." In reality, "It is gratuitous and inexorable." (1989, 92) The view that inflicting pain can be useful in extracting confessions or information in interrogations is not well supported, contrary to widely held beliefs.

The lack of human interaction does not just inflict temporary harms. Quite the opposite—the damage can be long-lasting. In terms of physical pain: at the International Symposium on Solitary Confinement, researchers and formerly incarcerated individuals made it clear that the damages outweigh any benefits gained with solitary confinement, notes research associate Tiana Herring. She observes that recent studies show that time spent in solitary confinement shortens lives, even after being released, and there are other ways solitary causes irreparable harm (2020).

Herring points out one of the ways solitary confinement is particularly dangerous. She says, "Prisons and jails are already inherently harmful, and placing people in solitary confinement adds an extra burden of stress that has been shown to cause permanent changes to people's brains and personalities. In fact, the part of the brain that plays a major role in memory has been shown to physically shrink after long periods without human interaction." (2020)

At the other end of the spectrum is the mental aspect of pain. It can cause effective immunity to those subjected to extreme isolation, points out Herring. For example, although those in solitary account for 6–8% of the prison population, they make up nearly half of those committing suicide. (Herring 2020) Those are sobering statistics and need to be taken seriously. Being placed in solitary should not open the door to abuse and mistreatment.

Justin D. Strong et al. reports that solitary confinement has been associated with psychological distress, such as anxiety, depression, paranoia, and aggression. And no wonder. Prisoners who spent time in solitary confinement were three times as likely to suffer post traumatic stress than those who had not. (Strong et al. 2020) This adds to the reasons for seeing solitary confinement as a substantial risk compared to being in the general prison population.

In light of the harms of solitary, it is not surprising that the United Nations considers solitary confinement for more than fifteen consecutive days to be torture. That is not always recognized in evaluating the harms of the practice. This may be affected by the lack of public exposure of policies in prisons and detention facilities. They are out of the public eye and, therefore, not given much, if any, attention. This is especially the case for those held in solitary in Supermax prisons. The "worst of the worst" get little sympathy.

12.3 The Evil of Separation

The second component of evil is fear of separation. Separation is not in itself evil, Noddings observes. (1989, 95) It can be good in certain circumstances, but have harmful results when misused. Nodding points out that some separations are "clearly good," as when our children go off to college or when someone in great pain finally dies. (1989, 95)

On the other hand, "Physical separation that induces emotional pain uncompensated by a sense of fulfillment, relief, or other positive affect is clearly evil to the one who experiences it." (Noddings 1989, 95) With solitary confinement, separation is at its most extreme. Those who have suffered it regard the experience as much worse than physical pain. Think of the lack of human contact when cut off from a community or other people. The effects of the segregation and isolation is almost impossible to imagine. Self-destructive behavior is a common response to the isolation—much like caged animals attacking themselves in despair.

Human contact is vital to mental health and should be considered when evaluating the (few) advantages and (many) disadvantages of solitary confinement. And the effects on the greater society should also be factored in—as John Stuart Mill would recommend (see Chap. 5). The harms of such separation should not be overlooked.

Studies by Keramet Reider et al. reported in *American Journal of Public Health* (2020) showed clinically significant symptoms of depression, anxiety, or guilt among half of the research sample. They had disproportionately high rates of serious mental illness and self-harming behavior compared with the general prison population. Additional symptoms included social isolation, loss of identity, and sensory hypersensitivity.

Noddings points out the "anxiety of meaninglessness" that goes with the evils of separation and helplessness. (1989, 100) For instance, consider the effects of the loss of control over one's own activities and environment. Noddings contends that the loss of meaning does not begin in a separation from ideas, but in a separation from people and ordinary life. The neglect of relation, she asserts, is in fact a basic evil. (1989, 100–101) The social dimension of our lives is necessary for our well-being.

12.4 The Evil of Helplessness

Noddings observes that pain is not the only or greatest evil. The third component of evil—helplessness—taps into a loss of control. Our autonomy feels stolen, out of reach. She argues that our sense of identity then suffers. For example, "to be helpless when one wants to act or, worse, when one feels that one *must* act—that is an evil." (1989, 93) She puts it this way:

> One sort of helplessness affects us as evil—the helplessness that thwarts our emotional sense of being able to or wanting to accomplish something. This helplessness generates anger, frustration, and anxiety; we cannot recognize our true selves in the situations that induce this feeling. (1989, 93–94)

Obviously, this impacts our mental health. No wonder inmates felt trapped in emptiness or in a tomb, lost and forgotten. Research suggests that the widespread use of solitary does not achieve its intended purpose. It does not make prisons, jails, or the community safer, and may actually make them less safe. Prison researchers and advocates Kayla James and Elena Vanko note that solitary confinement can have many adverse effects on people inside and outside corrections and detention facilities. This deserves close attention. It also provides compelling reasons, they assert, for corrections agencies to swiftly and safely reduce—and end—its use (James and Vanko 2021).

Think about it: How can a person stuck potentially for weeks, years, or decades *not* feel utterly helpless? It is not like there are easy-to-use channels of appeal—although there should be. Control over the conditions of their imprisonment is closed to them. When you are the one without power there is not a lot you can do. That fact fuels the sense of helplessness—powerlessness leads to helplessness.

Restricting the maximum length of their isolation would alleviate the stress of their confinement. However, indefinite detentions were a reality for people held in prisons and detention centers in Iraq, Afghanistan, Guantanamo Bay, and elsewhere in the war on terror. As Noddings astutely observes, "When we think of people as enemies it is easy to put them outside the moral community, to devalue their moral worth." (1989, 198) As a consequence, "this devaluation permits us to treat them in ways that would be unthinkable if they were part of our moral community. (1989, 198)

If it is an "Us versus Them" situation, we should not be shocked that relations are strained, and mistreatment is unleashed. It lays the groundwork for oppression

Addressing helplessness, as in the case of solitary confinement, shines a spotlight on oppression.

Noddings cites the work of Paulo Freire, who remarks: "The oppressor is solidary with the oppressed only when he stops regarding the oppressed as an abstract category and sees them as persons who have been unjustly dealt with, deprived of their voice." (1989, 162) Noddings contends, "There must be a pedagogy for the oppressor as well as a pedagogy of the oppressed." (1989, 163) She points out Freire's argument that,

> Any situation in which 'A'objectively exploits 'B' or hinders his pursuit of self-affirmation as a responsible person is one of oppression [as Ivan Illich states]. Thus they should have both the understanding of suffering and the longing for freedom…" (1989, 166)

Both the oppressor and the oppressed deserve our attention. To change the role of the oppression in solitary confinement we need to look at the role of policy makers who put the practice into place and sustain it. Just looking at the oppressed only takes us so far. As Noddings remarks, "most people find it hard to admit their roles in maintaining such evils." (1989, 157) If they do not—and cannot—protest the continuation of solitary confinement, it is not surprising that inmates feel helpless to modify or eliminate it. The reality is that they have little recourse.

Sometimes individuals or groups, deliberately or carelessly cause physical or psychic pain to others, Noddings asserts. She sees this as moral evil—a harm that individuals inflict on other human beings. That said, "Much of the pain that surrounds us," she observes, "does not stem from the intentions of particular moral agents, however, but seems to be the result of our customs and social structures." (1989, 156) As a result, evils thus induced are hard to be considered preventable. Subsequently, she notes, "they often go unidentified for long periods of time." Most people then fail to see their part in maintaining such evils," she argues (1989, 156)

Noddings agrees with Freire that "an oppressor, desiring earnestly to help, must give up his or her privileged way of life and join the oppressed wholeheartedly." (1989, 161) There is only so much those oppressed by solitary confinement can do on their own. That is one aspect of their helplessness. To change the situation and overhaul the use of solitary, the oppressed, oppressors, and social structures will all need to be addressed. This is particularly the case given how widespread and entrenched is the policy.

12.5 Conclusion

Psychologist Albert Bandura observes that it is easier to commit horrors at a distance. People can detach themselves from both consequences and intentions when they cannot hear the victim's pleas directly. (Noddings 1989, 221 That needs to change.

If evil were directly associated with pain, separation, and helplessness, Noddings contends, we would see that the following constitute great moral evils:

1. Inflicting pain (unless it can be demonstrated that doing so will or is at least likely to spare the victim greater pain in the future).
2. a. Inducing the pain of separation
   b. Neglecting that the pain of separation follows or those separated are thereby dehumanized.
3. a. Deliberately or carelessly causing helplessness.
   b. Creating elaborate systems of mystification that contribute to the fear of helplessness or to its actual maintenance. (1989, 221–222)

Noddings has this to say: "Early on I rejected the notion long ago by Socrates, and recently by Hannah Arendt that evil is simply absence of knowledge or good." Instead, she observes, "Evil is a real presence, and moral evil is the result of trying to do something genuinely thought to be good or rationalized layer on layer in gross bad faith. Evil is thus bound up in disputes over good." (1989, 229–230)

Our task is to see what we can do to address the evil of solitary confinement so positive changes can result. Noddings says, "I want to recommend seriously that we guide our responses to perceived evil by policies of connection." (1989, 221–222) She continues: "Evil is real, and to control it we need to understand it, and accept that the tendency toward it dwells in all of us." (1989, 229–230)

Assuming that is the case, what are we to do to make constructive changes with solitary confinement? To address the pain, separation, and helplessness attached to it, we should take to heart Noddings recommendation,

> If we believe this, a primary purpose of education should be to reduce pain, separation, and helplessness by encouraging people to explore the nature of evil and commit themselves to continue the search for understanding. … appropriately educated people should ask themselves: Is there a different way to accomplish my goal? Is the goal *itself* evil or tainted with evil? What good am I trying to achieve? (1989, 229–230)

We can make a difference, if we look carefully at the components of evil entangled in the practice of solitary confinement and take steps to transform it. Yes, we can make a difference.

References

Herring, Tiana. 2020, December 8. "The Research is the most Clear: Solitary Confinement Causes Long-Lasting Harm," Prison Policy Initiative, https://www.prisonpolicy.org/blog/2020/12/08/solitary_symposium/

James, Kayla and Elena Vanko, 2021, April. *The Impacts of Solitary Confinement*. Vera Institute, https://www.vera.org/downloads/publications/the-impacts-of-solitary-confinement.pdf

Noddings, Nel. 1989. *Women and Evil*. Berkeley CA: University of California Press.

Reiter, Keramet, et al. 2020. Psychological Distress in Solitary Confinement: Symptoms, Severity, and Prevalence in the United States, 2017–2018. *American Journal of Public Health*. https://pubmed.ncbi.nlm.nih.gov/31967876/.

Strong, Justin D. et al. 2020, October. The Body in Isolation: The Physical Health Impacts of Incarceration in Solitary Confinement. 15(10). https://journals.plos.org/plosone/article?id=10.1371/journal.pone.0238510

Chapter 13
Claudia Card: The Atrocity Paradigm

Contents

13.1 Introduction

Philosopher Claudia Card sets out a theory of evil providing us with a valuable tool for examining solitary confinement and the harms it produces. She proposes a middle path between Kantian-Stoicism and Utilitarianism as a way to understand atrocities and cites three cases to illustrate her theory of evil. These are horrors on a grand scale. She focuses on three categories: mass rape, domestic violence, and atrocities of oppression. She is particularly concerned when victims are used to enable the oppression, as in the Holocaust and slavery. I will argue that solitary confinement falls in the third (oppressive) category of evil. Card's approach is useful for this analysis. We will start with an overview of her theory.

13.2 Ethical Framework

Card starts with a characterization of evil. "Evils," she posits, "are foreseeable intolerable harms produced by culpable wrongdoing." (Card 2002, 3) The nature of the harms makes evil stand out; they are on a different level in terns of their effects and

W. Teays, *Solitary Confinement*, Library of Public Policy and Public Administration 20, https://doi.org/10.1007/978-3-031-96566-1_13

importance. She asserts that evils tend to ruin lives or significant parts of lives. Her focus is on the act (the wrongdoing) and its effects (the harm), rather than putting the moral agent on center stage. What follows is that evildoers need not be evil people, though they may become so in time (2002, 4). It is the act—the wrongdoing—and the resulting harm that Card puts under the spotlight.

In her article in *Hypatia,* philosopher Maria Pia Lara says, "The concept of evil, Card claims, is worth preserving; it offers important insights into specific kinds of human actions, and the ways persons relate to one another. In her view, we cannot define evil in abstract terms." (Lara 2004, 187)

The two components of Card's atrocity paradigm are (culpable) wrongdoing and (intolerable) harm. Wrongdoing is the evil action, and harm is the intolerable effect. If the effect is not intolerable, labelling it "evil" would be inappropriate. Similarly, the action itself must result from a human catalyst, not from a destructive act of nature (earthquake, hurricane, tornado, tsunami, etc.). Natural events are not *evils* since they are not caused by moral agency. She points out that, "When not guided by moral agents, forces of nature are neither goods nor evils. They just are." (2002, 5)

As she puts it, catastrophes are not the same as atrocities; nor is death itself an evil. However, the manner of death (such as being murdered) can be an evil. (2002, 5) Furthermore, an epidemic of a fatal disease becomes an evil when people fail to prevent it or they play a role in the spread of the disease, as in giving blankets that spread smallpox to Native Americans. The failure to respond can turn a catastrophe into an atrocity. That is where wrongdoing comes in.

To be culpable, Card contends, we ought to have acted differently. For example, we would *not* hold someone responsible (culpable) for injuries resulting from a car accident caused by another driver, while we *would* hold an arsonist responsible for intentionally starting a fire in a drought-stricken forest.

The two basic components are the deed and the suffering. Neither one, by itself, is sufficient for evil; both components are necessary. In terms of moral theory Utilitarians emphasize the harm (the effect) and Kantians emphasize human will (the wrongdoing). Card sees her theory as intermediate between these two theories. She considers both harm and wrongful willing essential to evil. She notes that Kant locates evil exclusively in the perpetrator's character. (2002, 24)

Card contends that Kant views radical evil as subordinating morality to *self-interest*—the bottom of the pit as far as evil is concerned. (2002, 24) For Kant, but not for Card, evil has no connection to harm. The effect is not where he focuses his attention. Card thinks Kant's approach is inadequate. For that reason, she supplements his position with the Utilitarian emphasis on harmful effects. Her atrocity paradigm rests on the two footings of foreseeable wrongdoing and culpable harm. As we recall from Chapters 4 and 5, the Principle of Utility recommends choosing the act that maximizes social benefits for the majority of people.

It is helpful to note what Maria Pia Lara has to say about the perpetrator and the recipient of the wrongdoing and harm; namely,

> In my view, it is important not to lose sight of the role that agency plays in defining evil, for only with the idea that someone is choosing to perform cruel actions upon others can we

> properly define and identify an evil action. If Card is right, we also need to recover the sufferer's view. (Lara 2004, 187–188)

If we want to bring harm into the equation, we must include both the wrongdoer committing the intolerable act and the victim suffering the harmful effects. One thing Card recognizes that others may overlook is that the perpetrator is not necessarily an individual. It could be a group or an institution. As a result, an analysis of evil should include this larger domain—such as a prison or its guards and staff in the case of solitary confinement. Furthermore, in some cases the one suffering a harm may also be a perpetrator, thus in dual roles. Card cites the example of Nazi Germany, but cases closer to home as in detention facilities bear consideration.

As far as intentions go, Card observes:

> [A]n evil *intention* is a culpable intention to do someone intolerable harm, or to do something with that foreseeable result, even if the intention does not succeed. In an evil *deed,* the intention succeeds.... The intention to inflict torture is evil because of its aim, even if the motive was not sadism.... Analogously, an institution, law, or practice is evil not only when its purpose is inhumane... but also when it is reasonably foreseeable by those with power to change it that intolerably harmful injustices will result from its normal or correct operation (as many believe true of capital punishment). (2002, 20)

She adds,

> An agent's *motive* is evil if it is no accident that, when the motive is efficacious, evil results—that is, the agent would bring about harm that makes or threatens to make someone's life intolerable. It is no accident that evil results from efficacious sadistic desires. (2002, 21)

Card goes on to say that someone could justifiably be considered evil because of persistent evil motives or intentions or based on gross negligence or recklessness. (2002, 21) In terms of a community or an institution, some participants could be evil, while others not. It is a question of how much knowledge or ability to foresee options that each one has. Card explains:

> Among participants who are evil, culpability takes different forms. Some do not know because they do not want to and so refuse to think or inquire. Others know but also refuse to think about it because they are not sadistic—or they are squeamish—and thinking about it could produce major internal conflict.... Or they look on the bright side, or tell themselves that if they didn't do it, others would and might do it worse. Some participants may fail to identify a better alternative, despite a genuine will to do so. One whose evil intentions are ineffective can also be an evil person if the intention persists. (2002, 21–22)

Card argues that "Having in addition some good intentions is insufficient to distinguish those who are not evil from those who are. If an evil person must be utterly devoid of good intentions, or be the authors of no good deeds whatever, then, of course, there are no evil people." She thinks these distinctions show that evil people need not be evildoers (as intentions may fail) and evildoers need not be evil people (as evil intentions may be anomalous). (2002, 22)

Card considers Kantian ethics and Utilitarianism to be both incomplete and too inclusive, though both have humane ends. She thinks Kant was too focused on the wrongdoer to the neglect of the harm to victims and Utilitarianism was too focused on the sufferer, to the neglect of culpability. She asserts that the two theories working together offer an effective means of looking at evil. That is beneficial for looking at solitary confinement. Let's take a moment to see how.

13.3 Solitary Confinement

As noted above, the atrocity paradigm has the following components:

- Foreseeable intolerable harm
- Culpable wrongdoing

First: "Foreseeable intolerable harm" describes the effect of the evil action. Card points out that, "harm is what is most salient [in] describing atrocities." (2002, 9) Given what we know about solitary confinement and the harms its victims have suffered, we should not be surprised at its effects. The evidence of harm is overwhelming. Just look at the extreme isolation, the lack of human contact, and the failure to have even the briefest of interactions. This is where Utilitarianism bears recognition, with its focus on end goals and consequences. Keep in mind its recommendation that we try to achieve the greatest amount of social benefit for the greatest number of people.

Second: "Culpable wrongdoing" Card argues that an evil intention is a *culpable* intention to do intolerable harm, as in an evil *deed*, when the intention succeeds. An institution, law, or practice is evil not only when its purpose is inhumane, but also when it is reasonably foreseeable by those with the power to change it. (2002, 20) That is an important point. Since not all the members of a community or institution may have the power to change it, they may not all be evil people.

Culpability can take different forms, depending upon what the participants know or do. Think of different practices in prisons or detention facilities. For instance, wardens, guards, and staff may go along with an abusive practice devised or put in place by others if for no other reason than to ingratiate themselves with those in power. In oppressive situations this may be more common than we might think, particularly in places like the detention facilities Abu Ghraib, Bagram, and Guantanamo Bay, where abusive practices were widespread.

Card argues that someone could be evil not only for having culpable intentions but also for lacking decent ones or even failing to treat others with respect and dignity. In Card's opinion, "Evils manifest a lack of respect for humanity and for basic freedoms." (2002, 48) She points out that Kant sees evil in what we *do* or are willing to do rather than in what we suffer—the harmful effects.

Here's where Utilitarianism comes in the picture: "Utilitarianism seems to evaluate deeds as we would expect victims to do, with the focus on suffering." (2002, 54) The victim's perspective is vital for understanding the harm of evil deeds. One way to get a handle on that with respect to solitary confinement is to read the memoirs of victims like Albert Woodfox (who spent 43 years in solitary) or Moazzam Begg (who wrote of the abuse he suffered and detainee deaths he witnessed at Bagram and Guantanamo Bay).

Whether a person is culpable depends on what they knew or could reasonably have known—whether the person's choices were wrongful and how much control they had. Atrocities are shocking, Card says, because we expect better of people and of communities and institutions. She recognizes that too often criminal punishments such as a prison sentence have subjected convicted offenders to basic harms. (2002, 63) We see this with forced nudity, hooding, sensory deprivation, force feeding, stress positions, and solitary confinement, among other harms.

13.4 Kant's Notion of Radical Evil

Since Card integrates Kant's emphasis on the wrongdoer, it is not surprising that she turns to his view of radical evil. Kant sets out his theory in terms of three stages, with each more morally suspect than the previous one and all connected by an emphasis on *duty.* Duty is of central importance. Kant's good will is, as Card points out, the will to do one's duty for duty's sake. (2002, 77) Duty rules.

With each stage the role of duty becomes like a wet fish slipping from our grasp. Kant refers to the three stages as "the natural propensity to evil in human beings." (2002, 76) The stages are as follows:

- *Weak will.*
- The first stage of evil is a lack of strength of character in not abiding by one's own principles. In this first stage we have a sense of the right thing to do even if accomplishing it falls short. Our weakness of the will results in our doing wrong because of a lack of willpower. Those who act wrongly from weakness instead of principle may be more appropriately seen as *evildoers* than as evil people Card contends.
- *Morally Impure Motives.*
- In Kant's second stage of evil, we act from mixed—morally impure—motives. At this stage we do the right thing for the wrong reasons. Impurity, Kant contends, is more dangerous than weakness because "it begins a process of corruption in the will." It sets the person on a slippery slope to not relying at all on duty. (2002, 76)
- *The Bottom of the Slippery Slope—Self-interest.*
- In Kant's third stage of evil, we are down in the moral muck. Here it is that "We now subordinate the requirement of duty to the pursuit of self-interest. Only at this point is it quite clear that a radically evil will has emerged." (2002, 77)

All the stages show a tenuous hold on duty. Kant makes it clear that we are each responsible for our own duties and the wrongdoing that follows when we don't give duty its moral significance. Kant's perspective is that, "In acting wrongly, we accord our desires or inclinations more importance than duty." (2002, 77) "Bad idea," Kant would say.

Card is critical of Kant's theory of radical evil. Lara says why:

> Taken as a whole, Kant's theory of radical evil is unsuitable for Card's "atrocity paradigm" because Kant thinks of evil as the way in which we subordinate the requirements of duty to those of self-interest. Finally, he states that we can do evil only because we have an interest or an inclination. Instead, Card puts forth the possibility that evil can be done merely for evil's sake alone, out of pure cruelty. (2004, 189–190)

Card emphasizes that Kant locates evil entirely within the will. (2002, 94) This is a position Utilitarians would reject. She notes the following about Kant's perspective:

> Although Kant's good will is the will to do one's duty for duty's sake, there is, on his view, no such thing as the will to do wrong *for its own sake*. A radically evil will is not analogous, in that way, to a good one…. We do wrong for the sake of an interest or inclination, not for wrongness' sake. Doing wrong for its own sake would be, according to Kant, diabolical, not human. Human beings, he maintained, are never diabolical. (2002, 77)

Card cites Kant's reliance on his second Categorical Imperative—the Humanitarian Principle—which defines moral wrongdoing "as [the] failure to treat human beings having dignity, as ends in themselves." (2002, 81) Kant contends that a principle is immoral "if it fails to respect humanity in *anyone's* person." (2002, 84, my emphasis) "When we wrong others, we fail to treat them as equals." That is "we fail to place the same value on their rationality as on our own." (2002, 95)

This results in a power differential, as in the case of the warden and guards versus inmates—as, for example, in a Supermax prison like Pelican Bay, or the interrogators versus detainees in a detention facility. Showing respect is in short supply when it comes to the oppressors and the oppressed.

Card further notes that "Kant's theory of evil draws helpful distinctions among perpetrators but is deeply deficient in its recognition of harms." (2002, 82) The simple matter, says Card, is that the two components of wrongdoing and intolerable harm are both necessary to a theory of evil. "What distinguishes evils from ordinary wrongs is the element of intolerable harm." (2002, 101) You cannot omit either and have the theory be as powerful as it could be. Both components are vital.

13.5 Conclusion

We see the importance of the two-pronged theory of evil—the atrocity paradigm—with the use of solitary confinement. The practice was instituted years ago and has been maintained up to the present with a variety of applications. This much is true: it has affected thousands of people—from juveniles to adults. The wrongdoers are both the individuals that sustain it and the institutional policies that hold it in place. That they are culpable is a view that Card would take.

Although many support the use of solitary, its harmful effects have been recognized. The work of Solitary Watch and other activists has publicized the misuse and human costs. The harms are significant and long overdue to be modified or eliminated altogether.

Let's put it in perspective. Many bad experiences, notes Card, may be unpleasant but are not really harmful. For instance, cheating on our taxes and shoplifting are both wrong. They are morally bad but calling them evil would be overkill. (2002, 101) Card explains: "Conduct is morally bad when it is *culpable* and wrong. It becomes evil when it also foreseeably deprives others of basics needed for their lives or deaths to be tolerable or decent." (2002, 102)

Card insists that it is the harm, rather than the culpable wrongdoing, that distinguishes evils from other wrongs. (2002, 102) Examples of evil practices that she cites are genocide, slavery, torture, domestic violence, and rape. Because prolonged solitary confinement has been regarded as torture (for example by the United Nations) we can consider it an evil practice. That being the case, it is time we put an end to it.

References

Card, Claudia. 2002. *The Atrocity Paradigm: A Theory of Evil*. New York: Oxford University Press.
Lara, Maria Pia. 2004. Autumn. *Hypatia* 19 (4): 186–193. https://www.jstor.org/stable/3811062.

Part V
Principles and Recommendations

Chapter 14
Principles and Ethics Codes

Contents

14.1 Introduction

Fortunately, there are excellent resources that provide guidance regarding solitary confinement and torture. These are: the Nelson Mandela Rules, and principles and ethics codes of the Medical Association, the Declaration of Tokyo, the American Medical Association, the International Council of Nurses, the Istanbul Protocol and, lastly, Physicians for Human Rights.

Bioethicist Steven H. Miles points out that,

> There are a set of professional codes, that are endorsed by the American Medical Association and the World Medical Association, that describe doctors' duties not only to avoid participating in torture, directly or indirectly, but also a duty to document it and to report it, going outside the chain of command if necessary. (Beck 2014)

What Miles expects of medical personnel needs to be emphasized: By no means enable abuse, falsify records, or fail to report and document mistreatment. No "dual loyalty" justifies such dishonesty. And let us not forget—the United Nations considers more than 15 consecutive days in solitary could be torture. Such prolonged

W. Teays, *Solitary Confinement*, Library of Public Policy and Public Administration 20, https://doi.org/10.1007/978-3-031-96566-1_14

extreme isolation can cause permanent harm. Whenever possible, medical personnel should intervene to stop torture and do all they can to treat injuries and address physical, mental, and psychological harms.

Think of examples from detention facilities like Bagram, Abu Ghraib, Guantanamo, and CIA black sites, where detainees have been subjected to torturous conditions such as sleep deprivation, extremes of hot and cold temperatures, beatings, stress positions, sexual assault, forced feeding, and other indignities. Forced hooding has been a common fixture at many detention centers and prisons. Examples of astonishing brutality in the CIA's interrogation program can be found in *The Senate Intelligence Committee Report on Torture* (2014). There we see that doctors, nurses, and other medical personnel did not all behave admirably. They have professional duties to guide their behavior and set limits on relationships with colleagues and patients. Moreover, they should treat their patients with dignity and provide adequate healthcare. This is affirmed in the following—the Nelson Mandela Rules.

14.2 Nelson Mandela's Rules

In 2015, the United Nations General Assembly adopted the Nelson Mandela Rules. Andrew Gilmore, then-Assistant Secretary-General for Human Rights, offers this overview:

> The Rules are based on an obligation to treat all prisoners with respect for their inherent dignity and value as human beings, and to prohibit torture and other forms of ill-treatment. They offer detailed guidance on a wide variety of issues ranging from disciplinary measures to medical services. For example, they prohibit the reduction of a prisoner's food or water, as well as the use of instruments of restraint that are inherently degrading or painful, such as chains or irons (2019).

The Rules consider solitary confinement a measure of last resort. Mandela, who spent 27 years in a South African prison, found solitary confinement to be "the most forbidding aspect of prison life. There was no end and no beginning; there is only one's own mind." (as noted by Gilmore 2019) According to the Rules, the relationship between health-care professionals and prisoners is governed by the same standards that apply to patients in the community. (Gilmore 2019) We can see the importance of those standards in the following:

Basic Principles of the Nelson Mandela Rules

1. Prisoners must be treated with respect for their inherent dignity and value as human beings.
2. Torture or other ill-treatment is prohibited.
3. Prisoners should be treated according to their needs, without discrimination.
4. The purpose of prison is to protect society and reduce reoffending.
5. The safety of prisoners, staff, service providers and visitors at all times is paramount. (Penal Reform International 2016)

Let us now get an overview of expectations of major professional organizations regarding health professionals and torture and its application to solitary confinement. We will look at key points of the World Medical Association and the Declaration of Tokyo, the American Medical Association, the International Council of Nurses, the Istanbul Protocol, and Physicians for Human Rights.

14.3 The World Medical Association

The World Medical Association (WMA) takes an uncompromising stand against torture and roots their position in terms of human rights. It puts forward these key points:

> Torture is one of the most serious violations of a person's fundamental human rights. It destroys dignity, body and mind and has far-reaching effects on family and community. Freedom from torture is a universal and fundamental human right for all as guaranteed under international law and defined in the UN Convention Against Torture. However, its practice remains alarmingly widespread, particularly in places out of public view.
>
> The WMA unequivocally condemns any involvement of physicians in acts of torture, whether active or passive, as a severe infringement of the ethics and human rights law. (WMA 2018a, b)

This is in line with the United Nations General Assembly Principle adopted on December 18, 1982, setting out an expectation for all medical professionals:

> It is a gross contravention of medical ethics… for health personnel, particularly physicians, to engage, actively or passively, in acts which constitute participation in, complicity in, incitement to or attempts to commit torture or other cruel, inhuman, or degrading treatment. (Human Rights Library 2018)

To summarize, the WMA considers torture and other cruel and degrading acts to be an explicit violation of human rights. It is significant that the debilitating effect on human dignity as well as harm to the victim's family and community is also highlighted.

The impact of torture extends far beyond the level of the individual. As a result, any involvement, whether passive or active on the part of health professionals, is to be condemned. It is also important to point out, as does the WMA, how widespread is the practice and how much of it lies outside the public eye.

> The World Medical Association's Declaration of Geneva is a modern restatement of the Hippocratic values. It is a promise by which doctors undertake to make the health of their patients their primary consideration and vow to devote themselves to the service of humanity with conscience and dignity. (United Nations sec 60)

Liberty rights should guide us in our ethical decision-making about how detainees and prisoners are treated, and the role doctors can play in sustaining just policies and practices.

For instance, both the patient and the doctor have the right to refuse force-feeding. Inmates also have the right to refuse medical experimentation.

Furthermore, justice dictates respect for persons and protection from harm—not to mention honoring self-determination. We might also note the "Respect for Persons" principle spelled out in the U.S. Navy's guideline about human experimentation. It is as follows:

> *Respect for Persons*: The rights, welfare, interests, privacy, confidentiality, and safety of human subjects shall be held paramount at all times and all research projects shall be conducted in a manner that avoids all unnecessary physical or mental discomfort, and economic, social, or cultural harm. (Secretary of the Navy 2006)

This guideline reflects the values that underscore Immanuel Kant's and John Rawls' goal of universalizing human rights (see Sects. 3.3 and 3.5). The Navy's guideline also calls for respect for privacy and confidentiality, as well as avoidance of economic, social, or cultural harm. These latter duties are important to point out, given the problems that have arisen. For instance, doctors and psychologists have violated privacy using patients' medical information in developing interrogation methods. Subsequently, phobias such as fear of insects, fear of snarling dogs, or fear of the dark have been used in interrogations. In addition, cultural harm has regularly occurred with disrespecting religion and the mistreatment of sacred texts such as the Bible and the Koran.

14.4 The Declaration of Tokyo

The WMA Declaration of Tokyo was adopted in 1975 and revised in 2016. It sets out guidelines for physicians concerning torture and other cruel, inhuman, or degrading treatment or the punishment of detainees and prisoners. Of utmost significance and influence, the guidelines in abbreviated form are as follows:

WMA Declaration of Tokyo's Key Points (WMA 2022)

1. The physician shall not countenance, condone or participate in torture or other forms of cruel, inhuman, or degrading procedures, whatever the offense and whatever the victim's beliefs or motives.
2. The physician shall not provide any assistance or knowledge to facilitate the practice of torture or other forms of cruel, inhuman, or degrading treatment.
3. When providing medical assistance to detainees or prisoners who could later be under interrogation, physicians should ensure confidentiality of all personal medical information.
4. Physicians have the ethical obligation to report abuses, where possible with the subject's consent, but in certain circumstances where the victim cannot express him/herself freely, without explicit consent.
5. The physician shall not use nor allow the use of medical knowledge or skills, or an individual's health information to aid any interrogation, legal or illegal, of those individuals.
6. The physician shall not be present during any procedure during which torture or any other forms of cruel, inhuman, or degrading treatment is used or threatened.

7. A physician must have complete clinical independence in deciding upon the care of a person for whom he or she is medically responsible. No motive shall prevail against this higher purpose.
8. Where a prisoner refuses nourishment and is considered by the physician as capable of forming an unimpaired and rational judgment concerning the consequences of refusing nourishment, he or she shall not be fed artificially.
9. The World Medical Association encourages the international community, the National Medical Associations and fellow physicians to support the physician and his or her family in the face of threats or reprisals resulting from a refusal to condone the use of torture or other forms of cruel, inhuman, or degrading treatment.
10. The World Medical Association calls on National Medical Associations to encourage physicians to continue their professional development training and education in human rights.

14.5 The American Medical Association

The position of the American Medical Association (AMA) is congruent with that of the WMA. It also sets out a clear statement opposing the participation of doctors in torture, whether actively or passively.

Opinion 9.75 of the AMA Code Asserts the Following Ethical Principles:

1. Physicians must oppose and must not participate in torture for any reason.
2. Physicians must not be present when torture is used or threatened.
3. Physicians may treat prisoners or detainees if doing so is in their best interest, but physicians should not treat individuals to verify their health so that torture can begin or continue.
4. Physicians who treat torture victims should not be persecuted.
5. Physicians should help provide support for victims of torture and, whenever possible, strive to change situations in which torture is practiced or the potential for torture is great (AMA 1995).

It is noteworthy that the AMA sets forth a moral duty on the part of the physician to oppose torture and not take part in any way. It is also important to prohibit doctors from even being present as a bystander when such brutality is enacted or threatened. This guideline has the effect of eliminating any question of complicity with what is taking place. Staying silent is not an option.

Note also that the AMA allows physicians to treat torture victims, but only if it is not in the service of allowing the torture to continue. That frees physicians to put their skills to the service of beneficence and nonmaleficence (see Sect. 4.2) However, it assumes physicians can make that determination, which may not be possible. Here's where the command to "Do no harm" comes in: If it is unclear to the physician how to do good in the context of torture, at least do no harm. If you can use your medical expertise to help the torture victim that is good—if not, do no harm.

Ideally, it would be advisable to have an added guideline specifying what path to take if it is unclear if the torture has ended or if more lies ahead.

Thirdly, it is commendable that the AMA looks to protect physicians who care for torture victims, so they are not persecuted for lending their help. This latter duty can create challenges, particularly if treating torture victims could be seen as complicity. Therefore, it is vital for physicians who *do* treat torture victims to make their opposition known and take steps to bring the practice to light.

"The physician's most important role is that of healer, and that role is seriously compromised in situations of torture and coercive interrogation," asserted AMA President Robert M. Wah in December 2014, criticizing doctors who assisted the CIA in torturing suspects. (Viebeck 2014)

14.6 The International Council of Nurses

The International Council of Nurses (ICN) sets out a similar expectation—and one couched in a duty to the Nursing profession. Specifically:

- ICN strongly affirms that nurses should play no voluntary role in any deliberate infliction of physical or mental suffering.
- The nurse's primary responsibility is to those people who require nursing care.
- Nurses have a duty to provide the highest possible level of care to victims of torture and other forms of cruel, degrading and inhumane treatment, and should speak up against and oppose any deliberate infliction of pain and suffering. (1989, rev. 1998)

As far as guidance goes, ICN seeks to provide access to confidential advice and support in caring for prisoners subjected to torture. Also, all levels of Nursing education curricula should recognize human rights issues and violations, such as torture. ICN's position is that:

> Violations of human rights are pervasive, and scientific advances have brought about sophisticated forms of torture. Nurses are sometimes called upon to perform physical examinations before prisoners' interrogation and torture, to attend torture sessions in order to provide care, and/or to treat the physical effects of torture. (Human Rights Library 1998)

The nurse's professional and ethical duty regarding torture is to the care of victims, but not only that. They also have a duty to let their opposition be known by speaking up and taking action. This latter duty should be explicit, given the prevalence of silence on the part of doctors and nurses against torture.

Commentators point out that doctors and nurses provide credibility for the policies and practices in which they take part. Hopefully, this results in their internalizing the two principles of nonmaleficence and beneficence, so they can play a leadership role in seeking justice. When others look to them for guidance, that guidance should be morally defensible.

14.7 Istanbul Protocol: Obligations To Prevent Torture

The Istanbul Protocol, also known as "The Manual on Effective Investigation and Documentation of Torture and Other Cruel, Inhuman, or Degrading Treatment or Punishment," was developed in 1999. As noted by Physicians for Human Rights,

> [It] is the first set of international guidelines for documentation of torture and its consequences. The Istanbul Protocol provides a set of guidelines for the assessment of persons who allege torture and ill treatment, for investigating cases of alleged torture, and for reporting such findings to the judiciary and any other investigative body (PHR 2017a).

Stated in the Istanbul Protocol are the obligations that States must respect to ensure protection against torture. These include: "Taking effective legislative, administrative, judicial, or other measures to prevent acts of torture. No exceptions, including war, may be invoked as justification for torture." (United Nations 2004, sec. 10)

The Istanbul Protocol affirms the Hippocratic Oath's emphasis on nonmaleficence. This is made explicit by the statement that Western medical values have been dominated by the Hippocratic Oath and similar pledges. In particular, "The Hippocratic Oath represents a solemn promise of solidarity with other doctors and a commitment to benefit and care for patients while avoiding harming them." (United Nations sec. 60) This spotlights three values, those of solidarity, beneficence, and nonmaleficence; thereby linking to Beauchamp and Childress's four principles of Western Bioethics (autonomy, nonmaleficence, beneficence, and justice) and reinforcing their importance (see Sect. 4.2).

The manual also has a promise to keep confidentiality. This underscores patient autonomy, and the Hippocratic Oath's duty: "Whatever, in connection with my professional practice or not, in connection with it, I see or hear, in the life of men, which ought not to be spoken of abroad, I will not divulge, as reckoning that all such should be kept secret." The Istanbul Protocol asserts:

> These four concepts are reflected in various forms in all modern professional codes of health-care ethics. The World Medical Association's Declaration of Geneva is a modern restatement of the Hippocratic values. It is a promise by which doctors undertake to make the health of their patients their primary consideration and vow to devote themselves to the service of humanity with conscience and dignity. (United Nations sec. 60)

Keep in mind that there is a strong connection between concepts of human rights and healthcare ethics. The central tenet is "the fundamental duty [is] always to act in the best interests of the patient, regardless of other constraints, pressures or contractual obligations." What follows from this is that "All health professionals… are judged to be guilty of misconduct if they deviate from professional standards without reasonable justification." (United Nations sec. 51)

Under no circumstances—including "dual loyalty"— is enabling torture a reasonable justification for abandoning professional ethics and, therefore, being guilty of misconduct. Health professionals should never lose sight of this.

14.8 Physicians for Human Rights

Physicians for Human Rights (PHR) has been active in working for change and directing doctors to use their medical knowledge and skills to bring acts of torture to light. As PHR (2017a, b) states in its section on anti-global torture,

> Despite the absolute prohibition of torture in international law, it continues to be practiced in more than 100 countries, from totalitarian regimes to democracies. Countries frequently justify the use of torture as a necessary means to extract confessions, identify terrorists, and obtain intelligence critical to preventing future violence. Convictions are difficult to achieve because torturers have become adept at inflicting suffering through methods that leave few physical marks.

Doctors and nurses play a vital role. In uncovering the systematic use of torture. Physicians for Human Rights points out, "Health professionals can detect signs of physical and mental abuse that are not evident to traditional investigators." (2017a, b) They can then help expose attempts to hide evidence of brutality and, with that, the ethical travesty that was committed (PHR 2017a, b).

14.9 Conclusion

We need to support organizations like Physicians for Human Rights that focus on ways physicians can work together to oppose torture and know what to do when evidence suggests that individuals have been victims of torture.

It is one thing to be aware of the ethical codes of one's profession but quite another to hold those codes and honor them as a moral duty. The work of Physicians for Human Rights, Solitary Watch, the United Nations, and other professional organizations emphasize the value of working together to effect change. Collaboration matters. It can be a powerful vehicle for bringing problems to light and making an affirmative difference.

The knowledge that over 100 countries in the world have practiced torture shows that change is in order. The professional perspectives, as we have seen, make clear the importance of opposing the degrading treatment and abuse of other human beings. They also make it clear that doctors cannot abstain from taking part in torture. They should also bring torture to light and expose those guilty of misconduct. They are morally obligated to report abuse and torture.

In light of the principles and the professional duties we have examined, there is no excuse for inaction on the part of health professionals.

References

American Medical Association. 1995–2024. *Code of Medical Ethics Opinion 9.7.5*. https://www.ama-assn.org/delivering-care/torture.

Beck, Julie. 2014, December 12. 'Do No Harm': When Doctors Torture. *The Atlantic*. https://www.theatlantic.com/health/archive/2014/12/do-no-harm-when-doctors-torture/383677/.

Gilmore, Andrew. 2019, July 18. The Nelson Mandela Rules: Protecting the Rights of Persons Deprived of Liberty. *UN Chronicle*. https://www.un.org/en/un-chronicle/nelson-mandela-rules-protecting-rights-persons-deprived-liberty.

Human Rights Library, University of Minnesota. 2018. *Principles of Medical Ethics relevant to the Role of Health Personnel*. http://hrlibrary.umn.edu/instree/h3pmerhp.htm.

Human Rights Library, University of Minnesota. 1998. *Links, ICN Position: International Council of Nurses; Torture, Death Penalty and Participation by Nurses in Executions* (1998). http://hrlibrary.umn.edu/instree/executions.html.

Penal Reform International. 2016. *Short Guide to the Revised United Nations Standard Minimum Rules for the Treatment of Prisoners (Nelson Mandela Rules)*. London, England: Penal Reform International. https://cdn.penalreform.org/wp-content/uploads/2016/01/PRI_Nelson_Mandela_Rules_Short_Guide_WEB.pdf.

Physicians for Human Rights. 2017a. *Documenting Torture Internationally*. Physicians for Human Rights, PHR.org. http://physiciansforhumanrights.org/issues/torture/international-torture.html.

Physicians for Human Rights, 2017b. *Torture*. Physicians for Human Rights, PHR.org, http://physiciansforhumanrights.org/issues/torture/.

Senate Select Committee on Intelligence. 2014, December 30. *The Senate Intelligence Committee Report on Torture*. Brooklyn NY: Melville House Publishing.

Secretary of the Navy. 2006, November 6. *SECNAV Instruction 3900.39d, Human Research Protection Program*. https://fas.org/irp/doddir/navy/secnavinst/3900_39d.pdf.

United Nations. 2004. Istanbul Protocol. https://www.ohchr.org/Documents/Publications/training8Rev1en.pdf.

Viebeck, Elise. 2014, December 12. AMA Rebukes Doctors for RoleIn CIA 'Torture'. *The Hill*. https://www.google.com/amp/thehill.com/policy/healthcare/227005-ama-rebukes-doctors-for-role-in-cia-torture%3famp.

World Medical Association, 2018a. *Torture Prevention*. World Medical Association. https://www.wma.net/what-we-do/human-rights/torture-prevention/.

World Medical Association. 2018b, April 18. *WMA Resolution on the Responsibility of Physicians in the Documentation and Denunciation of Acts of Torture or Cruel or Inhuman or Degrading Treatment*. World Medical Association. https://www.wma.net/policies-post/wma-resolution-on-the-responsibility-of-physicians-in-the-documentation-and-denunciation-of-acts-of-torture-or-cruel-or-inhuman-or-degrading-treatment/.

World Medical Association. 2022. *Declaration of Tokyo—Guidelines for Physicians Concerning Torture and Other Cruel, Inhuman Or Degrading Treatment or Punishment in Relation to Detention and Imprisonment* (adopted October 1975). World Medical Association. https://www.wma.net/policies-post/wma-declaration-of-tokyo-guidelines-for-physicians-concerning-torture-and-other-cruel-inhuman-or-degrading-treatment-or-punishment-in-relation-to-detention-and-imprisonment/.

Chapter 15
Recommendations

Contents

15.1 Introduction

We can see from the various moral principles set out by ethicists and international codes of medical ethics that the message is clear: Do not enable, condone, participate in, or otherwise support torture or the degrading treatment of others. This includes solitary confinement if in excess of fifteen days. Standing in the wings while others commit abusive practices is also morally repulsive and nothing any conscientious doctor, nurse, or other healthcare professional should take part in. Medical personnel may be coerced to provide legitimacy for torture in a prison, detention facility, or out in the field. Rejecting that is in everyone's best interest.

In terms of recommendations, strong sanctions and guidelines should be in place. Medical staff need to be clear in their own minds that mistreatment in any form is unacceptable. They must also avoid acts of deception, such as falsifying records, or staying silent while others lose their moral bearings. They should not lose sight of their fiduciary duties to their patients. And it needs to be understood that inmates, detainees and suspected terrorists are their *patients*.

Let us now turn to some key recommendations.

W. Teays, *Solitary Confinement*, Library of Public Policy and Public Administration 20, https://doi.org/10.1007/978-3-031-96566-1_15

15.2 Recommendations

1. *Justice. First consideration*: Goals and intended benefits. The philosophers and contemporary thinkers cited here put considerable importance on justice. There are good reasons for that. As Aristotle and John Rawls emphasize, justice involves fairness, and we should strive to treat those held in solitary confinement with the justice they deserve as fellow human beings. "An injustice involves a wrongful act or omission that denies people resources or protections to which they have a right," Tom Beauchamp and James Childress point out. (2009, 241)

   Basically, locking someone in an 8 × 10 cell and preventing contact with others is on a level of cruelty that is incomprehensible. How should we address the injustice? One step along the path to justice would be to allow visitors and some interaction with other inmates and staff. At least a degree of contact with others would make an affirmative difference in their lives.

   Another step would be the creation of an institutional review board to investigate and respond to concerns. They could set out an ethics code providing guidelines for improved staff-inmate relations. Jeremy Bentham saw a place for outsiders to come into the penitentiary and see what was going on. That included having access to the omnipotent observer—the supervisor.

   A third consideration is ensuring that inmates are allowed privacy and confidentiality regarding medical issues and personal effects. Finally, we should recognize their right to informed consent in medical experiments and medical care, including forced feeding.
2. *Beneficence. Second consideration*: Effectiveness—see where positive change can be achieved.

   Secondly, we should do a serious assessment of the living conditions— as currently they are abysmal. Furthermore, the duration of sentences in solitary are often stretched to excess. Minor violations of rules can result in lengthy confinement way out of proportion to the offense. There is also a great deal of variation in the race and age of the offenders. The racism in the different percentages—the disproportionality— of Blacks and Latinos in solitary compared to the general prison population suggests an underlying racism. That needs to change.
3. *Nonmaleficence. Third consideration*: Do no harm

   Both Nel Noddings and Claudia Card look at the components of evil. Noddings' three components of evil—pain, separation and helplessness—and Card's atrocity paradigm give us insight into the harms of solitary confinement. Clearly solitary confinement is beset with harms so debilitating that individuals are driven to self-destructive behavior crossing over to suicide. In Chap. 10, we considered whether suicidal inmates had the right to assisted suicide. That raises key issues about personal autonomy and nonmaleficence. If they cannot opt out, then the despair, depression, and rage will need to be taken seriously. There should be alternatives to 22–23 hours a day of solitude to ensure better living conditions.

4. *Rehabilitation: Fourth consideration:* Character development

   The bottom line is that character development is out of reach to someone being tortured.

   That can change only if they are not subjected to such extreme isolation and lack of social contact. As Aristotle, Rawls, Mill, Boylan and Noddings expressed, we are members of a community and to eliminate that is destructive to our humanity. We are social creatures, and our individual uniqueness and dignity is rooted in community soil. Fulfilling a purposeful life, as Aristotle would commend, contributes to our character development. Individuals trapped in solitary would find that fulfillment out of reach. Addressing that need is imperative.
5. *Compassion: Fifth consideration*: Guarding the guards.

   The warden and guards are members of the prison community, and the inhumanity and despair leave their mark on both the inmates and the staff. The staff have the advantage of being able to go home at the end of the day and see their family. However, the effects—the horrors— of witnessing the costs of those in solitary cannot be easily washed off. It goes home with them. As human rights activists Peter Hall and David N. Tornberg indicate it stains medical ethics. (2005, 1263)
6. *Political Action. Sixth consideration:* Limiting the use of solitary confinement.

   We cannot expect the victims and enforcers of solitary to solve all—and maybe not any—of the problems. It should not rest on their shoulders. Others, including concerned activists and members of the public need to help address the harms resulting from solitary confinement. Together they can pursue alternatives that can be to everyone's benefit.

15.3 Possible Sanctions and Penalties

Here are suggestions for addressing health professionals who enable or participate in torture or abuse:

- *Get input from different sources.* Bioethicist Jonathan H. Marks suggests the burden of ethical decision-making does not just rest on doctors' shoulders. "*Physicians should not be left entirely on their own to chart a course between these competing concerns*," he says. "A map should be drawn up with input from military and civilian personnel, physicians, lawyers, ethicists, and laity," Marks recommends. (2005)
- *Make reporting mandatory*, as with child abuse, suggest lawyer Henry Forbes Smith and human rights consultant Mark Freeman. (2005, 331) Personnel and management of detention centers would then face penalties for not complying.
- *The Task Force of the Institute on Medicine as a Profession and the Open Society Foundations finds that* secrecy allowed the unlawful and unethical interrogation and mistreatment and to proceed. (IMAP/OSF Task Force 2013, xxiiii)

- *Complicity is unacceptable.* As lawyer Henry Forbes Smith and human rights consultant Mark Freeman assert, "Those who perpetrate torture rely upon the silence and complicity of their colleagues." (2005, 332) The net of culpability should be widened to recognize all who have played a role, even if as a witness or enabler. Complicity in any form would then be scrutinized and assessed.
- *Sanctions or expulsion could be considered.* Marks points out examples of professional organizations taking action against doctors enabling torture by setting down sanctions. These include, for instance, those expelled by the Chilean Medical Society (for overseeing torture under Pinochet), a Brazilian medical council (for falsifying a death certificate of a torture victim), the National Medical Council of Uruguay (for abetting torture under a military junta), to South African sanctions (for not reporting or treating the torture of civil rights leader Steve Biko). (2005)
- Frank Donaghue of the Physicians for Human Rights calls for *psychologists and physicians who are involved to permanently lose their license.* (PHR 2017a) "The health professionals involved in the CIA program broke the law and shame the bedrock ethical traditions of medicine and psychology," states Donaghue (2017a). "All psychologists and physicians found to be involved in the torture of detainees must lose their license and never be allowed to practice again." If nothing else, they should face serious penalties.
- *Tighten the bolts on stiff sanctions—prosecute serious violations.* Hall and Tornberg agree that stiff sanctions are in order. In a letter to *The Lancet* they recommended that, "Every one of the 139 countries that ratified the UN Convention against Torture is obligated to either prosecute any suspects entering its territory or extradite them to a country that will." (2005, 1263)

Steven H. Miles notes the increase in holding doctors accountable for torture. He points out:

> Since 1975, the pace of punishing physicians has accelerated. During the 1980s, four countries (Argentina, Chile, South Africa, Uruguay) held physicians accountable for torture. As those four pursued new prosecutions, Brazil and Rwanda joined their ranks during the 1990s. Pakistan and Sri Lanka punished physicians in the first decade of the twentieth century. Since 2010, three more (Guyana, Italy, United Kingdom) have joined them... In the last thirteen years alone, 36 physicians have been punished for crimes against humanity, more than in the years 1975 to 2000 combined. (Miles 2014)

15.4 Conclusion

All these suggestions tell us that there is no shortage of ideas for transforming solitary confinement. The bottom line is that sequestering individuals and cutting off social interaction and communication is on a level of abuse that qualifies as torture. It is not just a form of punishment and, therefore, should be discontinued for most if not all of its uses.

Offenders, whether adults or juveniles, do not deserve the cruelty—and harms—of solitary confinement. Alternatives like those noted above, call for our consideration. It is long overdue to weigh the options. We have nothing to lose and everything to gain by setting the wheels of change in motion.

In his book on violence, Slavoj Zizek said "Sometimes doing nothing is the most violent thing to do." (2008, 216) It is time—long overdue—for that to change.

References

Hall, Peter and David N. Tornberg. 2005, October 8. A Stain on Medical Ethics [Letter to the editor]. *The Lancet* 366:1263.

IMAP/OSF Task Force, 2013, November. *Ethics Abandoned: Medical Professionalism and Detainee Abuse in the War on Terror, Institute on Medicine as a Profession* https://hrp.law.harvard.edu/wp-content/uploads/2013/11/IMAP-EthicsTextFinal2.pdf

Marks, Jonathan H. 2005. Doctors of Interrogation. *The Hastings Center Report* 35 (4): 17–22. http://www.jstor.org/stable/3528822.

Miles, Steven H. 2014, January 22. The New Accountability for Doctors Who Torture. *Health and Human Rights Journal.* https://www.hhrjournal.org/2014/01/the-new-accountability-for-doctors-who-utorture/.

Physicians for Human Rights. 2017a. Documenting Torture Internationally. Physicians for Human Rights, PHR.org. http://physiciansforhumanrights.org/issues/torture/international-torture.html.

Smith, Henry Forbes, and Mark Freeman. 2005. The Mandatory Reporting of Torture by Detention Center Officials: An Original Proposal. *Human Rights Quarterly* 27 (1): 327–349. https://muse.jhu.edu/article/178250.

Zizek, Slavoj. 2008. *Violence.* New York: Picador Publishing.

Correction to: Nel Noddings: The Components of Evil

Correction to:
Chapter 12 in: W. Teays, *Solitary Confinement*,
Library of Public Policy and Public Administration 20,
https://doi.org/10.1007/978-3-031-96566-1_12

The original version of Chapter 12 was inadvertently published with incorrect chapter title.

The chapter title "Noddings: The Components of Evil" has now been corrected to "Nel Noddings: The Components of Evil".

The updated version of this chapter can be found at
https://doi.org/10.1007/978-3-031-96566-1_12

W. Teays, *Solitary Confinement*, Library of Public Policy and Public Administration 20, https://doi.org/10.1007/978-3-031-96566-1_16

MIX
Papier aus verantwortungsvollen Quellen
Paper from responsible sources
FSC® C105338

If you have any concerns about our products,
you can contact us on
ProductSafety@springernature.com

In case Publisher is established outside the EU,
the EU authorized representative is:
Springer Nature Customer Service Center GmbH
Europaplatz 3, 69115 Heidelberg, Germany

Printed by Libri Plureos GmbH
in Hamburg, Germany